# Social Rule

## A Study of the Will to Power

By

## Elsie Clews Parsons

❋

**British Library Cataloguing-in-Publication Data**
A catalogue record for this book is available from
the British Library

# CONTENTS

# Social Rule

## THE SATISFACTION FROM THE SOCIAL CATEGORIES

IN any study of the relations between personality and social classification the queries arise why the social categories are alike so compulsive to the conservative-minded and so precious, why they are given such unfailing loyalty, why such unquestioning devotion? To offset the miseries 'they allow of or further, the tragedies they prepare, what satisfaction do they offer? Do they serve only as measures against change, as safeguards to habit,—this is the answer I once suggested,[1]— raising barriers between those most apt to upset one another's ways, the inevitably. unlike, the unlike in sex, in age, in economic or cultural class?

[1] Parsons, Elsie Clews, *Social Freedom*, p. 104, New York, 1915.

The social categories are no doubt a safeguard against the innovations personality untrammelled would be up to, and this protection is by no means a trifling social function; but the categories, it now seems to me, perform a positive as well as a negative service, they are an unparalleled means of gratifying the will to power[1] as it expresses itself in social relations. The classified individual may be held in subjection in ways the unclassified escapes. "Being women, eat crumbs!" a Chukchee may exclaim. A woman who dares talk back hears, "Since you are a woman, be silent!"[2] Besides, a would-be woman rebel is kept in her place the more easily if her rebellion mean "unsexing" herself, for both `sexes` will be arrayed against her.[3] Similarly a refractory junior will

---

[1] Since I shall make considerable use of this phrase, I would suggest that, like any other popular catch-word, it is harmless as long as it is recognised as a mere verbal convenience; but that it is a constraint upon thought when sociological authority is imputed to it. I therefore beg the reader to take it always in this discussion as a descriptive and not as an explanatory term. It is descriptive of that "general inclination of all mankind" which Hobbes calls "a perpetual desire of power after power that ceaseth only in death."

[2] Bogoras, W., *Mem. Amer. Mus. Nat. Hist.*, VII., Pt. II., 547, 548. Leiden and New York, 1907.

[3] Margaret Fuller once described very neatly the sometime value of sex classification to Anglo-Saxon husbands. "It has

not only be told that as a junior he should be seen and not heard, but, in recognition of the principle of seniority, he will find all his elders standing together against him. The poor man, the wage-earner, the slave, the illiterate, the commoner will have against him in any conflict with one of superior station all of the "upper" classes. The lawless, once pronounced a criminal, will have against him all the law-abiding.[1] Once the abnormal is labelled he is at the mercy of the normal. The more fixed the traits and functions of a ghost or god, the more assured and classified his supernaturalism, the more thoroughly is he in hand,

---

been inculcated on women, for centuries, that men have not only stronger passions than they, but of a sort that it would be shameful for them to share or even understand; that, therefore, they must 'confide in their husbands,' that is, submit implicitly to their will. . . . Accordingly, a great part of women look upon men as a kind of wild beasts, but 'suppose they are all alike.'" (*Woman in the Nineteenth Century*, pp. 150–1. Boston, Cleveland, New York, 1855.)

[1] The anti-national, I might add, or even the critic of national traits or trends will have against him all the patriotic. In this study I have not included an analysis of nationalism, but it deserves consideration in its aspect as a means of social rule. "I could not have controlled that convention," the president of a nationalist association said to me the other day, "had I not appealed from time to time to the national feeling. 'You say this' or 'you act thus,' I would exclaim, 'and you a Serb!'" "And you a Serb!" "And you a German!" "And you an

the more harmless or the more useful is he to his descendants or worshippers. A tutelary spirit, whether ghost or god, is expected to mind his business. He may not be neglectful, he may not be meddlesome or obtrusive. Once in Fiji Hocart tells us he was present with some natives who had met together in a house where the ghosts were to come to fetch away a dead man. One of the ghosts gave news through the medium that in ghostland he had just bought a boat. His living son, uninterested in this posthumous business transaction, bade his father begone. "I am a man, you, a ghost," said he; "I don't like you, I don't want to speak to you, go away."[1]

The preëminent function of social classification appears therefore to be social rule. In institutions

---

American!"—it is a very handy whip—in holding a convention, in getting votes, in going to war. The other day the President of the United States gave a fairly adequate account of the usefulness of the classified American: "If a man describes himself to me now in any other terms than those terms [Americanism], *I am not sure of him;* and I love the fellows that come into my office sometimes and say: 'Mr. President, I am an American.' Their hearts are right, their instinct true, they are going in the right direction and *will take the right leadership* if they believe that the leader is also a man who thinks first of America." (The New York *Times*, May 17, 1916.)

[1] Hocart, A. M., in *Folk-Lore*, XXVI. (1915), 132-3.

where subjection is most desired, institutions like the Catholic Church or like a modern army, classification is most positive and most patent. Classification is nine-tenths of subjection. Indeed to rule over another successfully you have only to see to it that he keeps his place—his place as a male, her place as a female, his or her place as a junior, as a subject or servant or social "inferior" of any kind, as an outcast or exile, a ghost or a god. Even to rule over yourself you must keep your feelings balanced, your thoughts from vagrancy.

Self-control is a means to controlling other people. So is self-classification. The feeling of having our class back of us gives us self-assurance. When we gratify our gregarious impulse, we enhance our sense of power. Similarly, by declassifying or demoting others or by suspending their regular classification, so to speak, we get a pleasurable sense of our own power. Such enhancement of the sense of power is part of the psychological explanation of the license of Saturnalia or Cronia, of women's days,[1] of the

[1] Many simple communities celebrate a day on which men and women exchange rôles. When New York was New Amsterdam such a day was kept. On *Vrowen Dagh* any girl could lash any

First of April. Slave owners, men, the Elders, all know that such suspensions of order or such institutional outbreaks but strengthen their rule. For somewhat the same reason employers of labour and navy and army officers are apt to be tolerant of week-end debauchery or of the sporadic sprees of river jack or sailor or soldier. Even the periodic returns the living allow the dead—the *anthesteria*, the all souls' nights—strengthen rather than weaken that sense of domination over the dead without which life to many would be intolerably fearful.

Demotion, putting into a lower class, is not only gratifying, it is a very common means of controlling a subject class. Subjugated men, for example, or men open to insult are sometimes classed as women. If the relatives of a Thompson River Indian killed by a strange tribe do not undertake an expedition of reprisal they are called women.[1] To so disgrace a Pulayan casteman that his fellows refuse him their society he is thrashed with the

---

boy she met with the cord whip she was that day entitled to carry. (Boese, J., *Public Education in the City of New York*, p. 18 n.)

[1] Teit, J., *Mem. Amer. Mus. Nat. Hist.*, II., 290, New York, 1900.

leafy garment worn by women.[1] Wishing to degrade the Delawares for violating a treaty, the Iroquois actually put skirts on them, "making women" of them,[2] as an Iroquois chief was once heard to jeer. The taunt of being only a girl is to us also fairly familiar.

Women may be taunted with being animals. When a South Slav woman asserts her superiority, to spite her, a man may declare that she is not after all a rib from Adam, for did not a dog run off with the rib God had taken out for her creation? Although God chased the dog, he did not recover the rib; he was able to grab from the dog only his tail, and it was out of this tail God had to make woman.[3] Analogously, adults may be called children, mere children; and a little boy or girl, "only a baby." Once when a native Congo trader wanted to snub the Rev. R. E. Dennett he called him, not an unfrocked priest, but merely "a small boy."[4]

[1] Thurston, E., *Ethnographic Notes in Southern India*, p. 453. Madras, 1906.

[2] Morgan, L. H., *The League of the Iroquois*, I., 329. New York, 1901.

[3] *Anthropophyteia*, I. (1904), 10–11.

[4] *Nigerian Studies*, p. 192. London, 1910.

The will to power and more particularly the will to power over other people is a more general character than we are quite aware of. There is an enormous amount of energy put to controlling or regulating human creatures, to keeping them in their place, to keeping them in order. In fact without exaggeration one may say that the bulk of our surplus energy, energy beyond that applied to sustaining life, expresses itself in ruling others.

A considerable part of energy spent on ruling or on social control goes into justifying the given means of rule or control; but with the resultant justifications we are not in this discussion concerned. We are not engaged in passing ethical judgment. Hence we can afford to disregard, as a rule, the rationalising or moralising almost every social act or belief is subject to. By this disregard we would not minimise the importance of the desire to moralise or rationalise. It is a highly significant social phenomenon, but, except as it is in itself expressive of the will to power, it is not pertinent to our analysis.

Our discussion will be a direct consideration of the more notable of the subject classes. It is in that way the facts first ranged themselves in my mind. In the course of my study, however, I began to notice the striking and amazing similarity of the disciplinary methods exerted over the subject classes. Segregation, a rule of silence or of posture, hair-cutting, dieting, killing, torturing, especially whipping, mutilating, branding or smearing, clothing, breeding, match-making or its preclusion, making work—these are the more conspicuous methods of social rule. To all of the subject classes from period to period or from group to group, they have been applied—to juniors, to women, to slaves and other "workers," to criminals, to defectives, to the lower animals, to the dead,[1] to gods, and, from an objective point of view, to oneself. It is to be hoped that monographs on these various methods of social rule will some day be written. Such a treatment might carry quite

[1] Even the dead, it is believed, can be killed. In Fiji, for example, if you die a bachelor, your ghost is likely to be slashed into bits. A Fijian tale is current of a chief who had encountered the ghost of an enemy and had killed him for the second and last time. [Mayer, A. G., in *The Scientific Monthly*, I. (1915), 29.] The Herero believe that a maggot which lives, they say, in the spinal cord becomes the ghost of the deceased. To kill the ghost, they fracture the backbone of the corpse. [*Folk-Lore Journal* (of South Africa), I. (1879), 55 ft.]

a far-reaching conviction about the character of
social rule.  A comparative study of the practice
of flagellation, for example, might lead the advo-
cate of corporal punishment to question whether
the belief that "the shortest road to a boy's moral
sense is through his cuticle"[1] is the main motive
in whipping boys; a like study of practices of segregation might suggest to certain moralists that
solitary confinement or ghettoes or the tenet that
woman's place is in the home were more than mere
means of safeguarding the law-abiding or the
virtuous, of protecting the home or purity of race.
Reviewing the forms of compulsory breeding or of
restricted feeding might arouse queries as to
whether anti-birth control measures had been
passed solely for the good of society, or whether
a minimum wage is opposed solely because it is
believed to endanger economic prosperity.  Indeed, not a few social formulas, not a few points
of view of accepted morality might find themselves
in jeopardy from such studies of the will to power.
In this discussion we are engaged, however, I would
repeat, neither in controversy nor in propaganda;

[1] Dictum of President Wilson, May 15, 1916.

we are engaged in analysis. And, let me add, with analysis from a single point of view, a view taken frankly and deliberately from one side.

In the course of this analysis I have had to assume some ethnographical information on the part of the reader and that amount of ethnological interest which is indispensable to a liberal education. Although rash, the assumption was necessary. To be enlightening, the sociological point of view of this study must be far reaching; it must include glimpses of many different societies. Although I have tried to hold to a comparative point of view, I have assumed that for the time our interest is concentrated in our own culture, and the discussion proceeds along this line of concentration. The discussion has therefore a social rather than a scientific character.

## JUNIORS

"YOU never asked me if I wanted to be born,"
is a form of filial reproach dear to the bud-
ding individualist. Were that kind of "smartness"
ever indulged in by offspring in primitive culture,
the taunt could be made even more telling. "You
didn't even leave my birth to nature. You prac-
tised phallic magic to bring me into existence or
you coaxed the gods to give me to you."

Unfilial the progeny, but his reproach may well
have a basis of fact. So often would-be parents
pray to the gods or make them presents or, like
the mother of Samuel, hold out to them the bribe
of dedicating to their service the child vouch-
safed. Most peoples are possessed of a deity of
reproduction who is believed to heed the petitions
of the childless, and one of the usual functions of
medicine-men or priests is to render women pregnant. It is, no doubt, we note in passing, one of
the most satisfactory expressions of the sacerdotal

will to power,[1] be the form it takes the natural act
of begetting, or pure magic individualistically
transacted, or a generalised ceremonial.

But a barren or even an impatient woman will
resort to supernaturalism without the intervention
of priest or god. There are endless recipes for
conception—brews and lotions, things to wear,
charms of all kinds. A South Slav will visit the
grave of a woman who has died in pregnancy to
beg from her her unborn child. The suppliant

[1] The function is arrogated sometimes by chiefs who retain a
priestly character. See note on the procreative power of holy
men in Parsons, E. C. (Main, John), *Religious Chastity*, pp.
297–9. New York, 1913.

The most achieved expression of this function noted is among
the Blackfellows of North Queensland and among the Akikuyu
of Rhodesia. The Kia medicine-man has only to practise will-
magic, merely ordering the woman to conceive. If the medicine-
man belongs to another tribe she will bear twins. On the Tully
River a neglected mother-in-law may send twins or triplets by
putting two pebbles or three where the woman sleeps. A congenital deformity is due, this tribe believes, to the wrong man
telling a woman to become pregnant. (Roth, W. E., *North
Queensland Ethnography*, Bull. V., 23. Brisbane, 1903.)

Among the Akikuyu any man who feels insulted by a woman
can work his spite against her by getting a medicine-man to
"bind" her, keeping her from conceiving by means of sympathetic magic. (Routledge, W. I. and K., *With a Prehistoric People*,
p. 268. London, 1910.)

Spiteful people in Montenegro may wish a girl on a bridal
couple. (Parsons, E. C., *The Old-Fashioned Woman*, p. 7.
New York, 1913.)

will eat a bit of the grass on the grave and carry some of the soil in her belt.[1]

Just as a woman will "do something" to have a child, having conceived one, she will "do something" to determine its sex or looks or disposition. For example, if a Banks Islander wishes her child to be a boy, she will eat the fruit of one kind of tree; to have a girl, she eats the fruit of another kind. Believing too that her unborn child acquires characters from the animals she may come across during pregnancy, she frequents the resorts of the animals who cause the traits she desires in her child. If she wants a light-coloured child, she will go to a place where there are light-coloured crabs. From these yellow crabs the child gets not only an attractive complexion, but a good disposition; from the hermit crab it gets an irascible and disagreeable disposition.[2]

There are many things too an expectant mother wishing to influence her child will keep from doing. Perhaps she will not eat the animals whose looks or nature it would be objectionable for the child

[1] Ploss, H., *Das Weib*, I., 690. Leipzig, 1902.
[2] Rivers, W. H. R., *The History of Melanesian Society*, I., 150. 153, Cambridge, 1914.

to acquire. She will keep from eating hare, for example, or venison lest the child have a hare lip or be timid like a deer. A New Britain islander will not eat the backward moving cuttlefish lest her child grow up a coward.[1] If she is prudent, the Bahaman negress will not "pity too much" a diseased or deformed person; her infant would be similarly afflicted.[2]

A pregnant Zuñi will not sprinkle bran over the floor of her oven lest the child be afflicted with pimples; like women in many communities she will not look at a corpse lest the child be stillborn.[3]

In Zuñi the father of an unborn child should not go hunting lest the child suffer the same injury he inflicts upon his quarry. Were he to shoot a prairie dog or a rabbit in its head or leg the child might be born blind or lame. In many other places too pregnancy taboos fall upon the expectant father as well as upon the expectant mother.

[1] Brown, Geo., *Melanesians and Polynesians*, p. 33. London, 1910.

[2] Personal observation.

[3] Parsons, E. C., "Zuñi Conception and Pregnancy Beliefs" in *Proceedings of the Nineteenth International Congress of Americanists*, December, 1915.

Although in all these taboos ideas of sympathetic magic are paramount, it is possible that the prohibitions also give parents a gratifying sense of their influence over the unborn child.

The pregnancy ceremonials so characteristic of the more primitive cultures undoubtedly gratify in some such way their performers. By their acts they are influencing, they feel, the well-being of the unborn as well as determining his future position in the world. It is at the pregnancy ceremonial among the polyandrous Todas, for example, that the father of the unborn child is decided upon; without the ceremonial the child is called *padmokh* and disgrace attaches to him for life. He belongs to no clan and he will not be allowed to perform the *pursütpimi* or pregnancy ceremonial himself, *i. e.* to become the legal father of a child.[1]

Pregnancy ceremonial serves not only to express the "interest" of the family connection in the unborn, it is a collective expression alike of impatience with nature and of reluctance towards

[1] Rivers, W. H. R., *The Todas*, pp. 322, 531, 546. London and New York, 1906.

nature, so to speak,—a means of meeting natural changes in a way to suit one's self, *i. e.* when one is "good and ready" and not before. These feelings of impatience and of reluctance enter largely into ceremonialism in general, and all epochal or crisis ceremonials may be considered expressions intrinsically of the will to control the change which has at last to be met. Birth, growth, decay, and death are all processes apt to be thought of in terms of crisis—we do not face them, we say, until they are upon us—and even then we face the changes they involve only to put them away from us as consummations. Our achievements in this respect take shape as ceremonials—birth rites (sometimes preceded by pregnancy rites, sometimes by pregnancy furtiveness or conventional secretiveness), puberty ceremonials or initiations, mating ceremonials or weddings, funerals and memorial ceremonials. Not only do these ceremonials help us clean the slate, they serve as shock-absorbers, as it were; they are a balm to our injured sense of control, to our feeling of lapsed control over life. They restore to us, by renewing our sense of

2

power, our self-respect.[1]   Let us consider the crisis
of birth.

A woman's behaviour during labour is held to
be influential upon the still undelivered child.  Her
self-control, it is quite widely believed by primitive peoples, affects his character and prospects.[2]
Has not the opposition in civilisation to women
taking an anæsthetic at childbirth based itself
largely on the argument that the unenduring
woman would give birth to weaklings?  "If his
wife was so soft as not to be able to bear a little
pain, what sort of sons was she likely to give him?"
queries the masterful East Prussian husband.
"A breed of shrinkers; a breed of white-skinned
hiders."[3]  At Motlav, in the Banks Islands, the

---

[1] Parsons, E. C., "Holding Back in Crisis Ceremonial,"
*American Anthropologist*, Jan.–Mar., 1916.

[2] Incidentally, self-control is agreeable to others.  In uncon-
scious self-protection people demand hardihood of women in
childbirth and, in many places, isolation.   Take the Chukchee
custom.  A woman in childbirth may not groan or give way to pain
in any way.  Alone, she has herself to cut the cord and put away
the placenta.  Were she to accept help, she would be mocked the
rest of her life.  Even her husband might be nicknamed derisively
"the helped one." (Bogoras, Pt. I., p. 36.)

[3] *The Pastor's Wife*, p. 228.  Pastor Dremmel was a scientific
farmer; hence, given this outlet for his will to power, in many
respects he did not "interfere with" his family or parishioners.—

expectant father performs a ceremonial shortly before delivery in which he gives two fathoms of money to his wife's brother that the woman's womb may be large and the child born strong.[1]

At Motlav and in East Prussia it is the father, not the mother, who would control the unborn child; at Motlav through his brother-in-law, in East Prussia through his wife, and here let us observe that the expression of will to power may be and often is of a vicarious nature. The foremost performer may be a mere puppet, either ceremonially or fortuitously. To non-combatants an army may bring satisfaction in this vicarious way. By punishing one's enemies and defeating evil-doers the gods may bring the same kind of vicarious satisfaction. The machinery of justice brings it and even abstract ideas of retribution or of fate. Admiration for the ruling classes, the gods, their priests, chiefs, judges, millionaires, etc., is a feeling, I think it is fair to say, akin to this vicarious satisfaction of the will to power. In-

---

This novel by the author of *Elizabeth and Her German Garden* is a remarkable bit of ethnography.

[1] Rivers, *Mel. Soc.*, I., 149-50.

deed the principle of vicariousness runs through and through all forms of social rule or ambition. We shall have to note it again and again.

It were impossible to enumerate all the practices resorted to for infants and little children to make them grow fast or properly, to make them strong, fleet-footed, good-looking, hearty, to give them quiet sleep, easy dentition, a good character, immunity from black magic, good fortune, "an education," professional qualifications, social advantages of all kinds. And to classify all such customs as expressions of the parental will is, I quite understand, to make a generalisation too sweeping to have any particular significance. Perhaps even nagging and fussing are too complex to be described merely in terms of parental wilfulness. And so I can merely say that the plasticity and docility of childhood afford excellent conditions for doing what you like with another person, even if it is only for his own good.

But there is another group of customs besides that of improving a child which may be less reservedly described as an expression of parental or familial tyranny—customs of child exposure or infanticide, and customs of pawning or selling or hiring out children. Among the Romans these customs were strikingly grouped. There stood in imperial Rome a column, the Lactaria, to which infants were brought to perish from exposure or to be adopted for purposes of slavery or prostitution.[1] Foundlings taken from the Lactaria or from near the Velabrum, another favoured spot, were sometimes mutilated—a limb would be cut off to qualify the child as a mendicant.[2] Consider the family custom in ancient Arabia. When an Arab father has tidings of the birth of a daughter, we read in the *Koran*, his face grows black and he is choked. He has to keep back his wrath. "He skulks away from the people, for the evil tidings he has heard; is he to keep it with its disgrace, or to bury it in the dust?"[3]

---

[1] These are not the only ends of adoption. They were not, as we know, even in Rome. But the practice of adoption—a widespread practice—appears to be largely due to the desire to have children to control, and part of the contempt commonly bestowed upon the childless arises from the sense of their impotency, not only impotency to beget or conceive, but impotency from having no offspring to order about.

[2] Payne, G. H., *The Child in Human Progress*, pp. 242-4. New York and London, 1916.

[3] XVI., 60-1. *Sacred Books of the East*, VI.

It is a vivid picture of the thwarted parental will Mahomet draws.

Among the Arabs infanticide was a paternal performance or privilege. Seldom is infanticide— or abortion—a maternal privilege, but very often it is not the father but the family elders who take the life of the newborn into their hands, its uncles or its grandparents. The elders, in turn, as well as the parents, may have to submit to the pressure of public opinion on the child's right to live. Not only because of sex, but through abnormality of various kinds, social or physiological, it may be deprived of that right. Illegitimacy, malformation, unusual delivery, albinism, dentition at birth, multiple birth, all are conditions pregnant with shame or misfortune or discomfort, not necessarily to the child, we must note, but to his family or to his community. Hence the resort to what is ever the simplest method of disposing of subject creatures—to nihilism, to killing.

In certain cultures infanticide under any circumstance is forbidden; but child service or child labour is a feature of every culture, existing side by side with the kind of parental devotion which

expresses, we have assumed, a parent's determination to improve his or her offspring or bring them
up well. In the same group, in the same family,
parents "do things" to their children and make
their children "do things" for them. Either activity may predominate in different classes in the
same group: in the poorer classes children do
things for their parents; in the richer, parents do
things to their children. In the same family it
is the younger children who are the more passive;
the older, the more active, a situation achieved in
its simplest form through "looking after the
baby."[1]

[1] In the circles where children are done by, little girls do not
serve of course as nurses, they are trained for maternity.

Agnes Repplier has recently made an amusing reference to
this education of "the future mothers of the race" (*Counter-
Currents*, pp. 171–2. Boston and New York, 1916), but curiously
enough she fails to point out that whether a child is trained for
citizenship as it is today or, as it was yesterday, for the family,
trained for character or trained for behaviour, its training is
probably in most cases primarily a gratification of its elders.
The "century of the child" is little but an euphemism. The
temper of twentieth-century education is strikingly like that
described by Plato. "Mother and nurse and father and tutor
are quarrelling about the improvement of the child as soon as ever
he is able to understand them; he cannot say or do anything without their setting forth to him that this is just and that is unjust;
this is honorable, that is dishonorable; this is holy, that is unholy;
do this and abstain from that. And if he obeys, well and good;

In circles possessed of "little mothers," in all primitive cultures, doing things to older offspring more or less ends with their adolescence. Then, if not before, the group Elders or leaders take the boy or girl in hand, performing ceremonial for their proper growth or prescribing conduct for it, educating them, breaking them in to conformity with group standards in all particulars of life. Habits of industry are laid, and sex habits and sex taboos. Youthful initiates are given friends for life. In the proper attitude towards the gods and their priests, towards chiefs, and particularly towards the Elders, in all these forms of morality, initiates are instructed.

They are instructed and at the same time they are, as we generally say, tested. More or less severe are the ordeals they are put through. These initiation ordeals are highly gratifying, I surmise, to those in charge. The initiation is as a whole a participation ceremonial, a means of classifying the youthful newcomer, and this act of classification, like all classifying acts, gives a sense of power.

---

if not he is straightened by threats and blows, like a piece of warped wood." (*Protagoras*, 325 c.)

Besides, in details, an initiation would appear in many instances to render its managers specific feelings of satisfaction. So much is done to the initiates,—their hair "is fussed with" or plucked out, their skin painted or scarified or tattooed, their teeth knocked out, their nails manicured, their sexual organs operated upon, their nose, lip, or ears bored, new clothes or ornaments put on. Moral traits lasting for life may be imparted to the initiate. During the ten days of the Hupa girl's ceremonial "especial care is taken that she does not use improper language or tell an untruth." If she does, she will continue untruthful, it is believed, throughout her life.[1]

Initiates are moralised. They may also be whipped or starved or segregated, sometimes with their fellows, sometimes in solitary confinement. They may even be ceremonially put to death.[2] Such "ordeals" are not so much tests, however we

---

[1] Goddard, P. E., "Life and Culture of the Hupa," p. 53, *Univ. Cal. Pub. Amer. Archæol. and Ethnol.*, I. (1903-4).

[2] This mock death is generally interpreted as a participation rite—*i.e.* the initiate must be made to break with the old life, his childhood life, before he enters on the new. This interpretation is well sustained, but is not this very break a display of power on the part of the initiation managers?

or even those who manage them may describe them, not so much tests[1] as expressions of social control.

To what degree is the control conscious? That were often, perhaps in most cases, difficult to estimate. When the middle-aged or elderly Blackfellow tells the youthful initiate that he must not interfere with the women, that if he even looks at a woman he will go blind or waste away, the instruction may be prompted a bit by marital caution. Similarly, Blackfellow taboos on diet may be dictated by greediness. The Tuscarora Indians said explicitly that but for the ordeals they put their young men through, the *husquenawing*, a course of starvation for weeks in the dark, they could never keep them under.[2] Contemporaneous disciplinarians of youth, they who insist that the most important trait in the young is "a capacity for doing what they do not want to do" may point out, if somewhat ingenuously, that this training of the will is not only the better for those

---

[1] For that matter, is not the test theory itself an expression of the desire to control?

[2] Webster, Hutton, *Primitive Secret Societies*, pp. 32-3. New York, 1908.

who are "coerced into self-control," but "for all those whose welfare will lie in their hands."[1]

Analysed, rationalised, or not, the desire to control a "youngster" is a major motive to disciplining or initiating him. Initiations may be considered indeed as great outbursts of the collective will over the individual[2] and in particular of the will of senior age-classes over junior. The age-classes are a peculiarly effective institution for social control. By this classification the junior need not be dealt with individually, but as a member of his class, and the proprieties of that class are binding upon him. He cannot cope with the argument, implicit or explicit, that all the other boys or young men are thus or do this or that. Since he wants to be one of them, he must conform. If it is against the rule for them to hold

[1] Repplier, p. 39.

[2] And not merely initiations of the young. Introduction into any group is likely to be an occasion for that group to indulge its sense of power. The form its indulgence takes ranges from inflicting bodily injury to imposing upon the initiate its creed or program. When a Mysore Holeya is given priestly rank his right ear is bored. When an outsider is taken into the fraternity of the Donga or Thieving Dasaris his tongue is scorched with a burning twig. (Thurston, p. 368, 402.) Harvard students extinguished cigars on the naked arm of a new member in their D. K. E. Society.

office or speak in council or appear unconstrained
in the presence of the older men, he too must be
mute and reserved.   In fact his own contemporaries will jeer and taunt him if he is too articulate
or too much at his ease.   "Fresh," "conceited,"
"stuck up," "putting on airs," are some of the
epithets our lads use to deride one who will not
keep to his place.   They as well as their seniors will
not tolerate such *breaks;* they will "take it out of a
fellow," they'll "fix" him, they'll "settle" him—
where he belongs.   So bent are they upon classifying the fellow,—the prig, the "mollycoddle," the
"grind," the "dude," the "swelled head,"—that
they do not observe they are merely putting him
where they have themselves been put—by their
seniors, by those who have determined what their
juniors shall eat and drink, what they shall wear,
what they shall say and what talk of, what they
shall read, what their interests in general shall be,
and what their occupations.

Here our immediate reference is to school boys
(and girls).   In the less primitive cultures it is in
schools the finer distinctions of the age-class are
most conspicuous, and the junior age-classes most

noticeably subjugated. At home a junior has some chance for self-expression. To deprive him of it, he is sent to school or, schools lacking, to serve in other households as page or apprentice. Away from home he belongs to a class, and class membership as usual involves class conformity. Apprentice or school discipline is maintained through the usual social instruments of subjection —through ridicule, privations, compulsory labour, imprisonment, and in some school systems through torture.[1]

Age-class distinctions are imposed by the Elders, but they are maintained by all. Juniors insist upon them, we see, for their own contemporaries, (each age-class upholds its distinctions, elders also for elders), but juniors even see to it that their elders are not remiss in their observance. Older people are *reminded* of their *dignity*, and bidden remember themselves and what they owe their age. To run, to dance, to wear clothes of certain cuts or colors, to flirt, to marry, are all activities

[1] Corporal punishment held its own in Anglo-Saxon schools until quite recently. For refinements on the simple methods of caning or cowhiding, refinements in the native schools of India, see Thurston, VI.

held incompatible, from group to group or from time to time, with advancing years. The Islanders of Torres Straits are so much ridiculed, if they are getting on in years, for having a child that they kill it.[1] Any child a Taveta woman may bear after the marriage of a daughter is put to death.[2] "Mother, when you get really old are you going to dress just the way you do now?" I once heard a little American ask with unconcealed concern his flighty, short-skirted parent.

Because the field of age-classification is open in part to almost everyone,—if there is almost always a senior to heed there is almost always a junior to direct,—the principle of seniority has held its own very persistently, its conservation has been so much to the interest of everyone, gratifying at some time or other everyone's wish to count. It is upon just this kind of diffusion of opportunities for self-expression through suppressing others[3]

[1] *Reports Cambridge Anthropological Expedition to the Islands of Torres Straits*, VI., 109. Cambridge, 1908.

[2] Hollis, Claud, "Notes on the History and Customs of the People of Taveta, East Africa," *Jour. African Soc.*, I. (1901–2), 110.

[3] A striking illustration of the operation of this principle and one pertinent to this general discussion is afforded by the treat-

that any principle of social rule must in the long run depend.

The principle of seniority brings concrete satisfactions of one kind or another to everyone, but to some of course it brings more than to others: it brings more, obviously enough, to those in the uppermost or "reigning"[1] age-classes; it brings more, likewise, to those to whom it is the unique or chief means of satisfying institutionally their desire to make 'themselves felt, to the young themselves and to women. Hence in the nursery, in school, in college, the claim of seniority is urgent,

---

ment of illegitimates, notoriously a persistently harsh treatment in spite of otherwise humane standards. The killing of illegitimates may be the only form of infanticide tolerated in a community, and their neglect or non-support suffered, when other classes of children are well provided for. By such discriminations the familial or parental will or, at any rate, the paternal will is recognised, as well as the will of the community, spiteful over the thwarting of its will the birth of the illegitimate implies.

Let me give in illustration the treatment of the Hupa child for whose mother no bride-price has been paid. Her child is called *tintailtcwen*, "he was made in the woods." He is an outcast and usually a slave. He is spoken to as the Hupa speak to their dogs. No money can be exacted for his death or injury. He is not permitted to enter the sacred sweat house. He can marry only with his kind. (Goddard, p. 56.)

[1] The reigning "age" is a Tavetan reference. Among the Wa Taveta and the Massai, social rule by very definite age groups is well illustrated.

and adages about respect or reverence for seniors are ever in high repute. Nor are disciplinary measures lacking, witness the fagging system of the English public schools, the irrepressible hazing of West Point or Annapolis, the custom in Taveta for the youths who are "made men" by circumcision to shoot off arrows with blunted tips at the uncircumcised boys.

Although European languages reveal the sometime rule of the Elders—what are senator, *seigneur*, earl, alderman, mayor,[1] but age titles?—although legislatures, courts, and high executive offices are for the most part still controlled by the elderly, although this very European War, it has been said, is an old men's war, nevertheless the rigid gerontocracy so characteristic of truly primitive culture is today obsolescent. And age-class boundaries in general are less clearly marked among us than among savages or than among our own not distant forebears. "You are mistaken about seniority counting so much, now-a-days at least," a woman said to me not long since. "In my family the

[1] Spencer, Herbert, *The Principles of Sociology*, II., 171, 173. New York, 1900.

older children have to give way to the younger, they are taught to look after the younger. And all I ever say to the children about older people is to listen to them because they have had more experience. Of course they must show good manners to older people. I have them stand when an older person comes into the room and I like them to be cheerful about fetching things when they are asked,—that sort of thing, you know."

"Yes, I know," I answered, and that sort of thing varies—a little. Let me read to you about it in the Islands of Torres Straits. It is good manners there for the boys to carry food and water to the men in their club-houses and to prepare their tobacco pipes. And I read: "When a boy left the fire at which his elders were seated he was instructed by his father as follows: 'When you go away you go along four-leg. By and by you been go little way, then you bend back. You no stiff yourself, my boy, or *maidelaig* [sorcerer] he make you no good. When you no see them big men [Elders] no more, then you stiff yourself."[1]

[1] *R. C. A. E. T. S.*, V., 306–7. Cambridge, 1904.

3

# WOMEN

THE rule of the Elders over the sex life of their juniors, whether it consists in regulating sex impulse or in ignoring it, this rule has ever been drastic, it is today in our own culture far more drastic than we realise. A great part of the history of marriage might be discussed from this point of view. For mating as an institution is planned largely for the benefit of the Elders and in many particulars it is primarily an expression of their will to power. I have little doubt that the Eskimo or Blackfellow parent or group Elder who betroths an infant or an unborn child is personally gratified, as we say, by the betrothal. The more noticeable motive in child betrothal or child marriage may vary—there may be a general desire to provide for offspring, or a kind of impatience to have the prospects of a son or daughter assured, or the betrothal or marriage may bring specific advantages to parents, a bride price or alliance

34

with another family, but, whatever the superficial or conspicuous motive, the interference on the part of the family Elders is at bottom, we need hardly question, to ensure their control.

In the fact that betrothal or marriage can be controlled more easily the younger the *fiancés* or the marrying, lies, I think, the main explanation of child betrothal and child marriage. But marriage at adolescence or later is still largely determined by parents or senior relatives,—witness the extent of marriage by barter or purchase or service. In these forms of marriage there is one aspect I would emphasise, namely, that the profit accruing to the family marrying off a girl is a subsidiary consideration. The main gratification in marrying her off is the sense of power it gives her seniors, a sense of power over her and over her suitor. It is for this reason primarily a marriageable girl is thought of as an economic asset. As a form of property, as a chattel, she is the more malleable. This aspect of proprietorship in living beings, proprietorship for the sake of malleability, figures in the conjugal relationship itself as well as in franker forms of slavery or of domestication. With your own you may do what you like.

And one of the things you are apt to like to do, if you are a forceful person, is to make creatures breed, not alone offspring, but animals, slaves, and, shall we say, friends, neighbours, fellow citizens, and sovereigns. Even the gods are required to beget and conceive. To satisfy this breeder's ambition, matchmaking flourishes in endless forms; the young are prepared for marriage[1] as well as married off; their own initiative in mating is harshly suppressed or penalised; celibacy is stigmatised, so are unauthorised child-bearing, unauthorised abortion, barrenness voluntary or involuntary, and the individual control of conception; child-bearing is accounted a moral, a religious, or a patriotic duty. Sometimes the extent of the duty is unrestricted, sometimes it is standardised. "Multiply and replenish the earth" command Jew and Catholic. "To be a worthy citizen, you must have four children at least,"

---

[1] Consider, for example, the rites of defloration and of circumcision. Whatever other meanings attach to these rites they have also to be regarded as preparatory to mating.

declares Mr. Roosevelt. "If you have three, you will receive land in the Campania," promised Julius Cæsar.

The self-determination in mating or child-bearing which leads to celibacy or unfruitfulness is discouraged, but the group itself reserves a right to decree chastity or barrenness. Sacerdotal chastity may be prescribed or chastity for the dead. A royal personage may be precluded from child-bearing, a male or female deity from sexual intercourse. Continence may be required of other professional classes, and the age at marriage may be specifically advanced. Dieri Elders, for example, order young men to wait until they have a full beard.[1] The Japanese feudal law of Satsuma forbade under pain of death any sexual relations with women until men were thirty.[2] American college faculties or trustees sometimes

---

[1] Howitt, A. W., *The Native Tribes of South-East Australia*, p. 183. London and New York, 1904. The Elders say that young persons marrying would be too much taken up with each other. The Dieri are without the ceremonial adjustment of a honeymoon whereby the early fervour is readily exhausted and the couple rendered sociable again.

[2] Carpenter, Edw., *Intermediate Types Among Primitive Folk*, p. 150. London, 1914.

forbid, not sexual intercourse, but marriage, under pain of dismissal.

When modern communities have to forego their control over child-bearing through losing the religious or the legal sanction[1] for a high birth rate, it is not at all improbable that they will prove highly arbitrary about sterilizing persons they may consider unfit. There may be a strong impulse to practise vesectomy, for example, against all "undesirable" citizens or against prisoners of war. Eugenics may be called upon to approve of operations upon anarchist women or upon feminists of a particularly obnoxious type.

I return to further consideration of what is as yet the more usual form of social control of propagation, control through marriage, and I would speak more particularly of marriage by service. Marriage by service is a particularly obvious expression of the seniors' desire to "manage." Far more gratifying than the economic service of the prospective son-in-law is his spirit of subservience. How severely it may be tested is well

---

[1] I refer to church and state pronouncements and laws against contraceptives.

illustrated among the Koryaks and Chukchees of North-Eastern Asia. The Koryak suitor has to serve from six months to three years. During this service his prospective bride is entirely inaccessible to him, intimacy were a sin. The girl may even leave home to live with relatives. Meanwhile her suitor is ill-fed, given a poor bed, not allowed to sleep late, and sent on exhausting errands. As the herdsman of the family he must pass his nights without sleep while the men of the family rest. His endurance, patience, and meekness are tested. In determining his work, the principal idea seems to be not his usefulness, but the hard and humiliating nature of his tasks.[1] The life of the Chukchee suitor is similar. He has to please the girl's father, her elder brothers, and other male members of the family. If one of the old people reproaches him and calls him names, he has to bear it patiently, he

[1] Jochelson, W., *Mem. Amer. Mus. Nat. Hist.*, vol. VI., Pt. II., pp. 735, 740. Leiden and New York, 1908.

Jochelson tells a story of how a Chukchee match-maker won the consent of the girl's father through rendering him a humiliating personal service, much as the gods are placated by acts of self-sacrifice, their pride gratified by manifest subserviency.

To make your subjection patent is a component of "good manners" to all "superiors," to all who have you in any way in their power or whom you would persuade of having power.

is even expected to agree. When the old people
are ill-tempered, they may starve him and deny
him shelter. This treatment may keep up for
months and even after he wins in the struggle to
get his girl he is expected to go on serving his
father-in-law for two or three years "*as long as his
joy in his wife is still fresh.*" [1]

From these Siberian instances as well as from
instances one might cite from many other parts of
the world it would appear that the sex life of men
as well as of women is regulated by their elders.
This fact has been curiously disregarded. And
yet whatever is a restriction upon the sex choices
and sex activities of women is almost necessarily
a restriction upon men. A high bride-price may
keep a young man from marrying, punishments for
adultery by women or limitations on their right
to divorce in order to remarry may affect men as
well as women, affecting men through the women
they would mate with. A double code of sex
morals is not always as clear-cut a dispensation
as moralists suppose. It is only when a class of
loose women, literally *loose* women, is recruited

[1] Bogoras, pp. 585–6. The italics are mine.

that men become at all independent of the sex
restrictions put upon family-controlled women.
Part of the opposition to a man marrying a prostitute is due to the will not to let him escape entirely
from that control which the Elders exert through
their control of women with family ties. To this
end, moreover, the sex life a man leads uncontrolled
by the Elders is made just as unpleasant by them
as possible. The less gratifying it is, the sooner
is a man anxious to enter into a family life, the
more he wants to get married, mating in accordance with the views of the Elders and of the
women who have accepted those views.

Women accept the views of the Elders on
mating and submit to their rule more unreservedly
and more docilely than men, a differentiation
going far to explain the existence of the so-called
double code. Whether the family rule requires
continence or incontinence[1] girls usually obey it.

[1] In East Central Africa a girl is told that unless she resorts to
the young men's house as soon as she is nubile she will die.
[MacDonald, J., in *Journal Anthropological Institute*, XX. (1892–
3), 101]; the Natchez told their daughters that only girls who had
disported themselves well with the youths would pass easily over
the narrow plank leading into the grand villages of the next world.
(Swanton, J. R., "Indian Tribes of the Lower Mississippi Valley

Nor from it at marriage is a woman as likely to be
set free as a man.  Her family keeps its hold over
her conjugal affairs.  In bride-selling communities,
for example, the bride-price is a kind of security for
good behaviour on the part of the bride.  Were
she to merit divorce her price would have to be
returned to her husband or his people.  In this
way a married woman remains accountable to her
family.  They control her through her bride-price.
Even in the absence of a bride-price, their consent
to her divorce[1] may be necessary.  An Omaha

and Adjacent Coast of the Gulf of Mexico," p. 94, *Bull. 43, Bur.
Amer. Ethnol.*).

In Chicago, in the neighbourhood of Hull House, mothers have
threatened their daughters that if they went to dance halls or out
to walk with strange young men they would give birth to devil-
babies to their lasting disgrace. (Addams, Jane, in *The American
Journal of Sociology*, July, 1914.)  More characteristically
American ways of threatening disgrace in order to exact continence of daughters will occur to the reader.

[1] Consent to divorce is not always, as we know, a familial
prerogative.  It has been usurped by rulers of all kinds, rulers
who, however they may differ in other respects, probably get from
this divorcing right the same kind of gratification.  No doubt
the Blackfellow elder who refuses to decree a divorce gets as much
satisfaction out of his obduracy as under similar circumstances
a New York judge or an English M. P.  The dictum that whom
God hath put together let no man put asunder must give an analogous sense of power to the god's representative.  Even a
democracy that professes belief in granting life, liberty, and
happiness to all may enjoy too much its control over mating to
grant divorce by mutual consent.

girl knew that if she married without her family's
approval she would not be able to get their consent
to a divorce. "Not so," her kinsmen would
retort, "still have him for your husband, remain
with him always."[1] Besides when neither law nor
custom requires a woman to heed her people in
getting a divorce, she may be greatly influenced
by them. "My mother says it would kill her if
I got a divorce," I once heard a sorely tried New
York woman exclaim. "How *can* I?" Eventually in this case the usurping old lady did not
have her way.[2]

[1] Dorsey, J. Owen, "Omaha Sociology," III. (1881–2), 262.
*Ann. Rep. Bur. Amer. Ethnol.*
[2] The way taken by parents to control the sex life of daughters
is not always of course to imply that independent action would be
murder. The following citation illustrates another very popular
method: "There is one occasion on which, perhaps, more than
on any other, daughters are apt to act in opposition to parental
wishes, which is, when they are about to enter into matrimonial
engagements. Is it not reasonable that they who have, with
infinite care, and perhaps at the sacrifice of health and strength,
nurtured you from infancy, and who have watched over your
opening years—is it not just and proper that their wishes should
be consulted, and their opinion treated with deference, when the
welfare of your whole life is at stake?" (Coxe, Margaret, *The
Young Lady's Companion*, p. 231. Columbus, 1846.)
Parental constraint may take still different forms. Among the
Todas the father of a married woman after consulting with two
Elders may sell her to another man. Neither her consent nor her
husband's is required. She is taken away by force. But the

Nor does a woman even without family interference become as she grows older more independent in sex affairs. From the dominion of her
family she passes under the dominion of her husband and, perhaps in addition, of his family. Even
when she goes on living at home and her husband
is serving for her or is more or less subject to her
household heads, even so, she is his to rule. She
waits on him and "does" for him. Few women
are institutionally as independent as Pueblo
Indian women and I am thinking more particularly
of Zuñi women. Zuñi women marry and divorce
more or less at pleasure. They own their houses
and their gardens. Their offspring are reckoned
of their clan. Their husbands come to live with
them in their family group. And yet Zuñi
women "look after" their husbands, look after
them quite as meekly, I surmise, as a wife after a

Elders may have to be bribed. (Rivers, *The Todas*, p. 525.) A
Fjort girl who objects to carrying out the matrimonial design of
her parents is brought to a fetich where she is "taken down" a
bit by hearing a voice say, "Are you then so beautiful that you
can afford to despise this good man on account of his ugliness?"
Thereupon her hands are tied and she remains a prisoner until she
consents. (Dennett, R. E., *Notes on the Folklore of the Fjort*, p.
97. London, 1898.)

husband among peoples where descent is paternal and the wife, a chattel. I recall a little incident I once saw—an elderly Zuñi coming indoors from threshing and bidding his elderly wife bring him water to wash his hands. Her compliance was not an act of graciousness, it seemed to me, it was the carrying out of an order.[1] She had the habit of doing what her husband told her.

Among us, this devoted wife would no doubt have been described as worth her weight in gold. Such a wife Martin Luther once described in even more glowing terms: "My rib, Kate," he writes, "is obedient and complying with me in all things, and more agreeable, I thank God, than I could have expected; so that I would not change my poverty for the wealth of Crœsus."[2] In all societies wives do in fact perform services that can not be bought. No slave or servant would care for you as well as a wife, and marriage is on the whole the most satis-

[1] Within the year another act of compliance cost this woman her life. She fell ill when she was camping out in the mountains gathering piñon nuts. The women with her quite properly advised warmth and rest but her husband insisted on driving her home; "alive or dead," he would get her home, he said. During the rough and cold drive back she died.

[2] Child, Maria, *Married Women*, p. 139. New York, 1871.

factory device yet worked out for the control of one adult by another.

Marital rule, like parental rule, displays itself along two main lines. A man *does things to* his wife—he has her cut off her hair or like the Galla, part it,[1] he has her blacken her teeth, he has her wear clothes befitting wedlock, clothes shabby or ornate as opinion goes, she is branded[2] for him or cut,[3] he has her forego ornaments or put them on, he has her live according to his station in life, he *supports* her. In patriarchal and semi-patriarchal cultures he *makes* her the mother of *his children*, in all but the most modern circles of modern culture he may impregnate her at will or

[1] Wakefield, Th., in *Folk-Lore*, XVIII. (1907), 324. A *divorcée* must wear her hair ruffled up again.

[2] On marriage an Ainu girl's tattoo is completed. "Her tattooed mouth must now speak only for her husband, and her tattooed hands and arms must henceforth work for him alone." (Batchelor, John, *The Ainu and Their Folk-Lore*, pp. 25–6. London, 1901.) Strictly speaking, I suppose prematrimonial improvements like this tattooing by the Ainu or like the foot-binding of the Chinese are a matter of parental rather than marital wilfulness.

[3] The Baganda believe that a woman who does not menstruate is a dangerous woman, a woman capable of killing her husband. The husband of such a woman always cuts her slightly with his spear before he goes to war, drawing her blood to ensure his safe return. [Roscoe, J., in *Journal Anthropological Institute*, XXXII. (1902), 39.]

he may keep her continent against her will. If
she is nevertheless wilful in this particular, he may
beat her or cut off her ears or nose or burn her
alive or shoot her with impunity or, like Master
Frankford in *A Woman Killed with Kindness*,
force her to suicide.

A "spotted strumpet," for her own good Mistress Frankford was shamed before her servants
and her children and then driven into exile.   In
many communities even for less offences a husband will chastise his wife.   A certain native of
Madura whose young wife was fond of gadding
about made her drag about a log chained and pad-
locked round her leg.[1]   This form of discipline is
applied in Madura to disobedient school boys and
apprentices.   Although such correction of the
young and of wives is rationalised as being
beneficial to them,[2] it no doubt gratifies the

[1] Thurston, p. 439.

[2] The doctrine about the moral need of obedience is a conspicuous outcome of such rationalising.   The will to power takes on
many disguises.   To obey for the sake of self, *i.e.* of character is
one.   To submit for the sake of society, for "the good of society"
is another.   To obey in order to serve God or to submit to God's
will is another.   The disguise in this type of submission is sometimes very slim.   The *Dabistán* instructs women to go three
times a day to their husband and ask his wishes.   Women

parent[1] or husband who administers it. Some forms of punishment render this view unquestionable. Take for example the treatment of an unfaithful wife in the Javādi hills of Southern India. "The young men of the tribe are set loose on her," after which she is put in a pit filled with filth.[2] Rape as a punishment for adultery is a practice elsewhere and it expresses, I take it, the sense of outrage a man feels when his will has been thwarted.[3] A wife's refusal to live with him may also be vexatious to a man. Among us all he can do is to bring a suit for the restitution of conjugal rights.

"must never, either by night or day, avert their face from their husband's command: which obedience on their part is serving God." (*The Dabistán*, p. 166. Washington and London.) See too p. 170.

[1] It is only a very modern disciplinarian who keeps assuring his subject that he himself gets no gratification from punishing. "It hurts me more than it hurts you," is the disclaiming formula.

[2] Thurston, p. 421.

[3] Verbal insults to a woman, a kind of verbal raping, are similarly indulged in by men who feel their sex prerogatives have been encroached upon. (*Cp.* Parsons, *The Old-Fashioned Woman*, pp. 289, 291.) The insulting restores to them, as it were, a sense of masculine power. Among other cases I have in mind an exploit of the medical students in the Blockley Almshouse in 1861. Irritated by the trespass of women on their profession, one day, to disconcert the women students, they brought into the lecture room a male patient entirely nude. (Meyer, A. N., *Woman's Work in America*, p. 165. New York, 1891.) The fear of antisuffragists that women voters would be insulted at the polls must be due to some such conception.

In Southern India in the Coimbatore hills he may see to it that his refractory wife is tied to a tree and the contents of a hornet or wasp nest emptied at her feet. After a few minutes the woman will be asked if she is now willing to live with her husband. In token of assent she has to lick a mark made on his back with fowl's excrement, and say: "You are my husband. In future I shall not quarrel with you, and will obey you."[1]

We have been speaking of real wilfulness in a wife, of real rebellion against being *sub potestate viri*. There is a kind of mock wilfulness or waywardness which is required of her, the pleasing kind of sex resistance we call modesty. It is particularly conspicuous during courtship or at marriage. A bride's reluctance or dismay is undoubtedly gratifying to the bridegroom or his people or to the kinsmen who are disposing of a woman.[2]

[1] Thurston, p. 420.

[2] Or of a man. There are "rape symbols" in connection with bridegrooms. Not uncommonly marriage propriety consists of imposing humiliations upon the bridegroom, making him feel he does not count for much. The Tavetan bridegroom, for example, has to play the part of a goat-herd. Only little boys or starving beggars serve as goat-herds and a more humiliating job can not be imagined by the Wa Taveta. (Hollis, p. 117.) The dignity of the bridegroom in civilization is not altogether respected.

4

The more she resists them or resists her bride-groom the more flattering is her final submission or conquest.[1] Hence non-resistance on her part, whether it is thought of in ceremonial terms or otherwise, is immodest, indecent, shameful. Incidentally we may note that refusal which has accept-ance in view, *i.e.*, a ceremonial refusal or denial may be gratifying to those making the advances. It enhances the sense of power the ultimate back-down gives them. Hence it is likely to be good manners to decline any offer or "honour" at its first making, even a post of command. It gives those who put you in command over them a sense that after all it is they who put you there. This is the reason, I take it, why at an initiation in Victoria the Blackfellow chosen sponsor vocifer-ously objects at first to accepting, declaring the honour far too great for him,[2] or why any well-bred Chinaman will accept an appointment to office by first declining it.

[1] The rape symbol is not of eighteenth century culture, but that a courtship was so often described in that period as a *conquest* is a fact belonging to the same complex of ideas or feelings.

[2] Smyth, R. Brough, *The Aborigines of Victoria*, I., 67. Melbourne and London, 1878.

We have been discussing what a husband does to or for a woman. The other line taken by the marital will to power we have already referred to, it is having a wife do things for you, further your convenience, be considerate of your needs, sexual and material, keep your house, spend your income or add to it, bring up your children, entertain your mates or guests or friends, perform the "social duties" you would evade, and in general look after your "interests." To be a "good" wife a woman must be satisfactory along both these lines, reconciling them discreetly and soberly. She must let her husband do things for her, she must depend upon him, gratifying his sense of chivalry, and she must also be a woman of character, able to represent him in the outside world, able to say with the Roman matron, *Ubi tu Caius ego Caia,* a woman in short you would not be ashamed of, a woman you don't have to leave at home or whom you would not blackball as a member of your club.

That conjugal rule is wholly marital needs hardly be said. A woman may do and often enough does things for or to her husband. She looks after his

health, his sleep, his digestion, his apparel, and
she takes care of him in this way, not because he
tells her to, but as she would for a child, a kind of
mothering which is, I surmise, a satisfaction of
her own will to power. It gives her a sense of
being needed, she says, of having a place in
the world.[1] Even the feeling that a man is
working for her, working not because she is
part of his equipment—the usual motive in
so-called work for women,—but because he is
truly her servant, even this feeling of domination I have seen entertained now and then by
women.

From the institutional point of view, however,
it is women who gratify men's will to power rather
than men, women's. There is as yet little or no
institutional provision for the bossing of men by
women. The henpecked husband is an object of
ridicule. So is the husband who so lets his wife
escape his control as, in that curious antique phrase,
to make him wear horns. According to Hindu
precept the man who shows love to a wife who

[1] To keep her place in the world, *i.e.*, to preclude becoming an
outcast widow, a Hindu bathes in turmeric water, a matchless
specific for longevity in husbands. (Thurston, pp. 366–7.)

constantly contradicts him becomes liable to censure himself.[1] The early German who let his wife strike him was likely to have the roof taken off his house by his critical neighbours. The only proper way to deal with such a wife, they held, was to make her ride backwards on an ass holding on by the tail.[2] Indeed everywhere the woman who eludes such retaliation, the woman who twists a man around her little finger, even the woman who plays neck to her man's head,[3] is only the de-institutionalised woman, the woman who in some way or other has cut loose from familial or conjugal conventions. In Gaina terms she is not a woman at all, but a "female demon."[4] Even the woman movement we have called feminism has not succeeded by and large in giving women any

[1] *Narada*, XII., 94. *Sacred Books of the East*, XXXIII.
[2] Goodsell, W., *A History of the Family as a Social and Educational Institution*, p. 196. New York, 1915.
[3] This figure of speech I take from the Rev. Eben Galusha of New York, one of the ecclesiastics who objected to the seating of the American women delegates at the Abolitionist Convention held in London in 1840. (*History of Woman Suffrage*, I., 56. New York, 1881.) The Rev. Galusha did not object to the rôle of the neck for women.
[4] *Uttarâdhyayana Sûtra*, VIII., 18. *Sacred Books of the East*, XLV. Such are women "who continually change their mind, who entice men, and then make a sport of them as of slaves."

control over men.[1]   It has only changed the distribution of women along the two stated lines of control by men, removing vast numbers of women from the class supported by men to the class working for them.

This redistribution of women may be of course just an incident of feminism.   It may be that this movement is primarily not concerned with the control of one sex by the other at all.   The main objective of feminism in fact may be defeminisation, the declassification of women as women, the recognition of women as human beings or personalities.

It is not hard to see why the classification of women according to sex has ever been so thorough and so rigid.   As long as they are thought of in terms of sex and that sex the weaker or the submissive, they are subject by hypothesis to control. Just as soon as women are considered not as creatures of sex, but as persons, sex regulations

[1] It tends in fact to lessen even those sporadic opportunities for backstair influence so precious to the old-fashioned woman. From the standpoint of success in controlling males the "lady" is more perspicacious than the "new woman."  In the lady's social system although backstair influence is hardly institutional it is not the illicit or immoral exploit the feminist would make it.

cease to apply. To preserve the application of sex regulations neither women nor men must forget for a moment that women are women. Their womanliness must never be out of mind—if masculine rule is to be kept intact. To be declassified is very painful to most persons and so the charge of unwomanliness has ever been a kind of whip against the would-be woman rebel. Not until she fully understands how arbitrary it is and how guileful, unwittingly guileful of course, will she cease to fear its crack.

The more thoroughly a woman is classified the more easily is she controlled. The vernacular phrase, a *new woman*, has the psychological significance so curiously attaching to popular phrases. The *new woman* means the woman not yet classified, perhaps not classifiable, the woman *new* not only to men, but to herself. She is bent on finding out for herself, unwilling to live longer at second hand, dissatisfied with expressing her own will to power merely through the ancient media, through children, servants, younger women and uxorious men. She wants to be not only a masterless woman, one no longer classified as daughter or wife, she wants a share in the mastery men arrogate.

This share has been and will be a sorry bone of contention between men and women. Men will cede to women only what by ceding gives them an assurance of power, like making an allowance to a wife or educating a daughter to citizenship,[1] or they will cede only what they consider has ceased to give mastery—just as they are now ceding the vote or the ecclesiastical profession or the Latin language or parental proprietorship.[2] And women will continue to find the campaign against sex discrimination or disqualification a more or less satisfactory outlet[3] for their energy. And so it

[1] As soon as men realise—and that day seems near—the field open to them not in educating women along the old line classically defined by Rousseau—to render men's lives easy and agreeable—but in educating women to hold men's social standards, some of the foundations of the present feminist movement will be shattered. Dissimilarity between the sexes and not similarity may be the new feminist war cry, feminists taking up the position now held by anti-feminists.

[2] Or just as German men opened their industrial guilds to women when the factory superseded the guild (Anthony, Katharine, *Feminism in Germany and Scandinavia*, p. 177, New York, 1915), or just as women were allowed to teach in the United States when learning ceased to qualify for political leadership.

[3] Not that masterful women will not find other outlets. Women satisfied by other outlets, outlets probably secured as early

will go—at least until a subordination of sex to
personality far more sweeping than we dream of
today comes to be. Given that subordination,
difference of sex will prove a stimulus between
personalities and a means of mutual aid. Without
such subordination it will be a source of antagonism and strife.

---

feminist gains, like public speaking or civic work, women thus
satisfied may prove the most active anti-feminists. Besides,
anti-feminism is itself an outlet for energy. The more vocifer-
ous anti-suffragists have been masterful women. Social obscu-
rantism has been known to offer opportunities for the will to
power.

## SLAVES AND SERVANTS

GIRLS get their training in womanliness as much if not more from their own sex as from the opposite sex. Nor are the older women merely passive instruments of education. Beneficiaries of the principle of seniority, they dominate younger women, just as the older men overrule the younger. Emancipated more or less by age from the subjection required of sex, older women appear not unwilling to inculcate sex submissiveness in their juniors as well as age submissiveness. "By night and by day" a Hindu mother-in-law expects to watch a young wife. The other wives likewise watch.[1] It is the older women who teach Wemba girls to chant at their nubility ceremonial:

> The husband is powerful within the hut
> We, the women, are merely as the chaff which hangs
>   from the roof.[2]

[1] *Brihaspati*, XXIV., 2. *Sacred Books of the East*, XXXIII.
[2] Sheane, J. H. W., in *Journal Anthropological Institute*, XXXVI. (1907), 156.

Disciplining girls in modes of feeling or behaviour towards men enlarges a matron's field of operation.

In this attitude of the older women lies a considerable part of the explanation of polygyny. It is usually the first wife who is the head wife and she is not unwilling to have younger women under her. We often hear indeed that in polygynous circles a woman asks her husband to take another wife—to lighten her labours, as it is said, to be at her disposal. If her superior rank as senior wife is clearly defined, it is not likely she will be jealous. As in the Hindu zenana, she will even watch over the younger woman in her husband's interest. Similarly, a man who lends his wife to a guest or a "friend in wives," to use the expressive Koryak term, is not jealous. It is his control over his wife that he values and that is made more manifest, rather than weakened, by lending her. Somewhat analogously a woman will give her handmaid to her husband to wive, as Sarah gave Hagar the Egyptian to Abraham, or as a woman I once knew was not averse to her husband "flirting" with ladies she approved of and under circumstances advantageous to her own "social position."

Gratification of the will to power enters into polygyny too from the husband's point of view. Polygyny may satisfy either his reproductive impulse or his will to breed. Besides, the supply of children of which polygyny is productive is subject in many societies to the *patria potestas*. Polygyny may also take on the character of an economic satisfaction. Where it is allowed, it is more or less peculiar to the older men. They alone can afford to buy or, in some cultures, to keep more than one wife. The possession of several wives is therefore a token of wealth and a source of prestige. Where wives are productive, polygyny is not only a sign, but a source of wealth. "I must take another wife," says an elderly Omaha. "My old wife is not strong enough now to do all her work alone." Part of her work consists in making articles for her husband to give away in order to secure to himself tribal honours.[1]

Under more complex economic conditions, with slavery or under the feudal or the wage system, the need felt by the elders of both sexes for polygyny

[1] Fletcher, A. C. and La Flesche, F., "The Omaha Tribe," p. 326, XXVII. (1905–6), *Ann. Rep. Bur. Amer. Ethnol.*

is lessened. A woman who is given a slave girl as part of her dowry or an allowance to pay for servants does not feel the need of a junior wife or concubine to afford her more leisure or prestige or to inspire her with the feeling of being mistress in her own house. Nor does a man who can keep both men and women retainers or employ labourers or clerks or stenographers feel the need of a harem—for social display. In want merely of sexual diversion it is more convenient for him to visit a house of prostitution[1] or to keep covertly a mistress. Considered by and large modern prostitution is part of the modern substitution of paid female service for involuntary conjugal service. More strictly speaking, the prostitute bears the same relation to the wife *in manu* as serf to slave.[2]

[1] Offsetting the conveniences of prostitution, conveniences that are continually threatened, as we have noted, by those who benefit from marriage, are certain inherent drawbacks. The relation can not satisfy the begetting impulse nor, outside of limited circles, can it be a means of social ostentation. And yet so manifest are its even simpler or crasser gratifications that it is referred to as "the necessary evil," the users of this catchword arguing that without prostitution, seduction and rape would vastly increase. Without slavery or serfdom, economy, it was once argued, would come to a standstill. The answer was free labour.

[2] See Reed, John, "The Rights of Small Nations," in *The New Republic*, Nov. 27, 1915, for a vivid picture of a transition from prostitute to wife in the Bulgarian oilfields.

The paramount duty of a slave, as of a wife *in manu*, is submissiveness; he must not oppose his will to his master's. Opposition entails punishment of various kinds, from minor deprivations to whipping, mutilation, death. The degree of the correction corresponds on the whole to the degree the owner feels he has been thwarted. Augustus is said to have had a slave crucified because he had killed and eaten a favourite quail. The Roman ladies must have been likewise highly exasperated when they tore their slaves' faces or stuck them with the long pins of their brooches. The correction of children and of women is undertaken more or less on the same principle of exasperation. With all three classes of course, slaves, children and women, the group at large may choose to curtail the power of the owner or master, decreeing that he shall punish only under certain circumstances or that of the use of certain penalties he may be altogether deprived. Although the British and American slave system was the most brutal on record slave owners were never allowed by the State to kill or maim their slaves openly at pleasure. Constantine decreed that slaves might be corrected only with a lash or slender rod, not, as once, with a cudgel. Manu decreed that sons and wives might be corrected with a rope or split bamboo and "on the back part of the body only, never on a noble part."[1] In many communities an adulteress may be killed by her husband only when taken *in flagrante delicto*. Modern states have usually deprived husbands of the right altogether, sometimes, like New York State, arrogating a milder punishment to themselves.

The submissiveness or subserviency of slaves means for the most part compulsory labour, its nature more compulsory than is the labour exacted of other subject classes, although of them all more or less forced labour is a characteristic condition. Child labour and wife labour[2] we have noted. Even when convicts[3] and prisoners of

[1] IV., 164, VIII., 299–300.

[2] To suggest considerations about wife labour aside from polygyny, I may refer to the nineteenth century English and American laws about a wife's earnings belonging to her husband and to the existent German law which gives the husband the right to forbid his wife to work for others if he considers that the home is being neglected. (Anthony, p. 179.)

[3] Criminals were enslaved among the Hebrews, the Hindus and the Chinese. (Westermarck, E., *The Origin and Development of the Moral Ideas*, I., 682, 685, 688, London, 1908.

war[1] are not enslaved, they are put to work without their consent or compensation; so, needless to say, are some of the domestic animals, and sometimes the dead, sometimes the gods. But the labour of all these controlled classes is not assumed to be as incessant as a rule or quite as involuntary as slave labour. More marked in the more voluntary

[1] Lecky, W. E. H., *History of European Morals*, New York, 1873. War captives have been generally enslaved—when not put into a kinship group or killed. Even when killed their ghosts are sometimes thought to be enslaved.

An excellent illustration of the display of power over captives is given by the case of some English prisoners taken in 1782 by the French, delivered over to Hyder Ally Khan, and sent to Seringapatam. Their things were taken from them, their heads were shaved and they were circumcised. Rings, the badge of servitude, were put in their ears. Several were taught dancing and forced to dance in woman's dress before Sultan Tippoo. Tippoo would cut off the noses and ears of prisoners caught escaping. (Thurston, pp. 385, 387.)

The world-wide torturing or mutilation of prisoners of war is a notable manifestation of the will to power. Its display by women is particularly interesting as one of the comparatively few institutional opportunities allowed women to work their will against men.

But even in this instance the will of women may be confined. It is said that a Chippewa woman would beg her husband going to war to bring back to her to kill a female, mind you, not a male captive. (Nieboer, H. J., *Slavery*, p. 51, The Hague, 1910.)

That women frequently appear to be less cruel than men may be due to the fact that the more conspicuous opportunities for cruelty are denied them. Given the opportunities, women do not seem reluctant to take advantage of them. To cite a comparatively unfamiliar example, the zenana women in Southern India have been said to strip the Kojahs or eunuchs in their zenana and make fun of their helplessness. (Thurston, p. 396.)

forms of labour is the principle of working by the piece, a principle which more than any other distinguishes free labour from slave, and which in transitions from slavery to serfdom is particularly distinctive. It is distinctive too in modern economy in determining the position of certain classes of salary earners in comparison with wage earners. To be master of your time, or even to have the illusion of it, is an emancipation often outweighing pecuniary considerations. In domestic labour, for example, other considerations aside, a woman would rather be an unpaid wife than a paid servant.

In return for his slave's labour and submissiveness, a slave owner assumes certain obligations, obligations in some communities far from light, obligations to support his slave, to provide for him in general, to be responsible to the community for the slave's conduct. Duty and obligation are legalistic terms, at least in this case; in psychological terms we may say that, as in the matter of conjugality, the greater a slave's dependence, the greater his master's gratification. Hence slave masters or mistresses have been known to be very

5

*good to* their slaves, just as men are to the women
to whom they are "lords and masters," or as
parents are to their own children, or women, to
their domestic servants.

Servants may acquire property and, unlike
slaves, as a rule,[1] dispose of it. As early as the
seventeenth century and perhaps before, English
servants were remembered in wills.[2] At this
period their wages, to be sure, were not high—
from 30 shillings to £6 a year. At this period the
spiritual and moral welfare of servants was also

---

[1] In ancient Rome the *peculium* of slaves was recognised. At
death, however, part or all of it reverted to the master. Public
or state slaves were allowed to dispose of half their goods by
will. (Lecky, I., 322.)

As a rule the subject classes are not given full property rights.
The dispossession of women and of minors is too common to
need particularisation. Equally common is the dispossession of
the dead even when they are believed to be able to appropriate in
Dead Land whatever is surrendered to them. In England until
1870 felons forfeited their property. It is only lately that perpetual franchises to foreign *concessionaires* in backward countries
have aroused among us any criticism.

Deprivations of property or restrictions in holding property
are readily explicable on the hypothesis that "the motive that
lies at the root of ownership is emulation." (Veblen, Th., *The
Theory of the Leisure Class*, p. 25. New York and London, 1905.)

[2] Slaves in Africa sometimes become their masters' heirs.
Among the Bayaka, for example, if the deceased leaves no heir,
his wives and goods pass into the possession of one of his slaves
who thus becomes a free man. (Nieboer, p. 431 ft. 1.)

provided for. According to a Massachusetts law of 1672 they had to be catechised once a week.[1] Mary Rich, Countess of Warwick, writes under date of Nov. 13, 1668: "After dinner I spent the whole afternoon in examining and exhorting my servants to prepare themselves to receive the sacrament. . . . I did much endeavour to bring them to a seriousness in the matter of their souls."[2] As for inculcating seriousness in behaviour a mistress or master relied not infrequently on cuffings and beatings. And yet, writes a modern commentator, "the servants of the seventeenth century showed a devotion to the family and its interests in happy contrast to the indifference of their successors of the present day."[3] The dependent are usually more capable of devotion than the independent.

Twentieth century servants are comparatively independent. In this country, unlike the indented

[1] Salmon, Lucy M., *Domestic Science*, p. 47. London and New York, 1897.

[2] Cited by Goodsell, p. 296. Over a century later concern over servants' souls was still habitual. See Defoe, Daniel, *The Family Instructor*, I., 173. Oxford, 1841. There are circles in England today where the practice survives of having the servants in to family prayers.

[3] Goodsell, p. 296.

immigrant servants of an earlier time, they may not be whipped either by master or magistrate. They may travel without a pass. Hotel keepers may take them in—if they are careful to separate them from the other guests. They may buy and sell. They may marry without the consent of their master. Unlike the servants legislated on in the French Constitutions of 1791 and 1795 or in the Hungarian Diet of 1847-8 they are not disfranchised.[1]

To a certain degree, however, servants are still closely directed or "looked after" by their employers. The master or mistress not only regulates the servants' work in detail, but also matters not necessarily connected with the work, the afternoon or evening "out," the hour to be in at night, the visitors they may receive, their sex habits. A servant's name, hair, dress, diet, tastes and manners are all more or less prescribed. I know a mistress who has changed her maid's name from Mary to Jane,—there is a "Mary" in the family. Another mistress calls every butler

[1] Salmon, p. 72, n. 1. Of comparative interest is the fact that among the Kafirs of the Hindu-Kush, slaves are sometimes elected to office. (Westermarck, I., 680.)

she engages "Thomas."[1]    Who would employ a
butler who wore a beard,[2] or a footman controver-
sial in metaphysics?    A taste for bright colours is
objectionable in a lady's maid[3] or a taste for beer
or for piano-playing in a parlour maid.    A coach-
man may not smoke while the carriage waits;
waiting on the table precludes laughing at a joke.[4]

[1] The social psychology of name-giving deserves study.    In
such a study the function of naming as a source of gratification
will appear significant.    It is generally arrogated by the ruling
classes, by the Elders, by husbands, by overlords, by State or by
Church.    At ceremonials, persons are apt to be renamed, an act
of assertion by the managers of the ceremonial.    Naming acts
attach to the subjection of many of the subject classes.    In
primitive culture there is more than a latent feeling that if you
know a person's name you are at an advantage, an advantage
denied you if you are a subject, or one at any rate you may not
make use of.    As naming brings the satisfaction of classifying,
so "calling names" partakes of the satisfaction of declassifying.
This is the reason, in part at least, why a Torres Islander speaks
of his wife as a ghost or as rubbish or excrement (Rivers, *Mel.
Soc.*, I., 195), or why children born under ominous circumstances
are often given contemptuous names, a form of self-depreciation
supposed to be pleasing to the gods.

[2] The Chinooks like so many other Indian tribes flatten the
heads of their infants, but this mark of aristocracy is forbidden
Chinook slaves.    (Nieboer, p. 431 ft. 3.)

[3] Among the Malays of Menangkabao slaves were not allowed
to dress in the same manner as free people, nor wear gold or silver
ornaments.    (*Ib.*)

[4] In Queen Anne's day, according to the scornful reference of
Thackeray, a lady would still joke with a footman.    But making
jokes for the amusement of a master is a form of service long
since out of fashion unless we consider the trick of asking "silly"
questions or naive questions, a trick sometimes encouraged in

The other day I saw placarded in large red letters in the hall of the top floor of a New York house, "The servants will not make any noise."

Some of the phrases peculiar to the lips of a mistress talking of her servants or to them are fairly indicative of her sense of control over them or her desire for it. "Meat once a day is quite enough for them," she grumbles, "Cereal is much better for them than eggs, but I can't get them to eat cereal." . . . "If I engage you, you understand you must wear a cap." . . . "I am very particular about the way you look," . . . "The kitchen door is locked at ten o'clock."[1] . . . "I

women and in children, an expression of such service. To be sure, also, funny stories are required of American orators.

To the student of the institution of the clown or Court jester I recommend for comparison the clown-making custom of the Blackfellows of Victoria. Men are taken forcibly by a chief, their hair cropped and plastered with white clay, their faces and bodies painted white. Then between the dances of the corrobboree they have to imitate animals and make various jokes. They are given presents of food—"tips." (Dawson, J., *Australian Aborigines*, p. 83. Melbourne, Sydney and Adelaide, 1881.) The "Delight Makers" of the Pueblo Indians also deserve study.

Does buffoonery tickle the sense of superiority, *i.e.*, of power in those it aims to "amuse"?

[1] In colonial Connecticut servants were not allowed abroad after nine P. M. (Salmon, p. 44.) "His time is yours," Defoe informs the master of an apprentice-servant, "and you ought to know how he spends it." (*The Family Instructor*, I., 230.)

don't allow my servants to have visits from men[1]—
you never know." . . . "I can't have outsiders
interfering with my servants—it is a great im-
pertinence." . . . "One thing I will not take
from my servants, a refusal to carry out my orders.
If they refuse, they have to go, I discharge them
on the spot."

The circumstances of discharging and of engag-
ing servants are sometimes rather crassly illus-
trative of domestic rule. The "reference" is a
potent little instrument of subjection. "I never
give a reference to any one who stays with me less
than six months." Woe to the impertinent one
who talks back,[2] she is sure to leave without a
reference. One mistress I know withholds the
wages of any servant who stays with her only
during the first trial week. The "restlessness" of

[1] Or from anybody. *Cp.* Salmon, p. 152 n. 1.

[2] "I won't be contradicted!" is a formula applied also to women,
to children, to the young men who are given a seat in council but
no voice, and, shall we say, to those criminals who, in one society
or another, have their tongues cut out.

On the other hand, to make people talk, to keep them from
"standing mute," to use an early English term for contempt of
court, is an assertion of power which has been supported in many
societies by innumerable forms of torture. A recent illustration
as applied to a "backward" people was the practice of the water
cure in the Philippines.

servants is often an attempt, I have thought, to assert themselves.[1]   The prerogative of "leaving" is at least theirs.   They are not the serfs their employer too readily assumes them to be.   They will give her notice, they will *show* her.

.They may attempt to "show" her too less radically by declaring she has asked of them some service it is not their place to do.   This is usually an effort rather futile and, I think, rather pitiful, to standardise their own labour, an effort their mistress finds so exasperating, however, that she invariably ascribes it to a disobliging nature. Had she herself risen in domestic service from being a maid of all work she might better understand that specialisation of labour is the main road away from slavery open to the domestic servant.

At other times resistance to my lady's rule takes a still more negative form.   The secretiveness that seems so strange to an amiable mistress,—the more *considerate* she is, the more strange it seems

[1] The restlessness of wives is somewhat analogous or, as it is sometimes called, the "instability of the modern family."   Getting a divorce, eloping, playing truant, deserting, going on strike, breaking jail, becoming a "free thinker"—one and all are acts, are they not, of running away, temporarily or forever, from the master?

to her,—that secretiveness is largely due to the wish not to be interfered with. To manage one's own affairs, one sharply realises if one is a servant, one must keep them to one's self. The mistress can't "boss" what she knows nothing about, it is safer not to let her know. Hence the quarrels, sicknesses, amusements, the griefs and joys of the servants are carefully hidden from the lady of the house.

Much of "that side of their life" as she calls it, she does not wish as a matter of fact to know about. The more impersonal servants are, the more exacting she may be in the matter of their service. The loss of opportunities to regulate them as individuals is offset by the greater opportunities to regulate them as members of a class, to set standards which, if they know their place, they must conform to. Hence class barriers of secrecy, of reserve, and of impersonality are kept up in domestic service to an extraordinary degree, to a degree incredible to one without experience either as servant or mistress. There is an archaic character to domestic service that has passed out of other social relations. Evidence of this character appears not only in domestic manners but in legislation, domestic service being excluded in several countries from their legal provisions for workmen's compensation, for a minimum wage and for a maximum day. In Germany the servant is subject to a special law, the *Gesinde-Ordnung*, which deprives her of all rights towards her employer, preserving "an old feudal relation which every other occupation has lost."[1]

In conclusion I query why women nowadays are so conservative of the custom of keeping servants—in spite of growing difficulties in getting them or keeping them.[2] Instead of simplifying their household arrangements so as to require fewer servants, women elaborate them in ways to require more. Labour-saving devices whether of organisation or of machinery women preclude as

[1] Anthony, p. 187.

[2] To Mrs. Gilman it is this circumstance, it is the very intricacy of the so-called servant problem, that will tend to eliminate the servant, or rather, the mistress class. I can not altogether agree with Mrs. Gilman. The more difficult the "problem," the more it will appeal to the ambitious American woman—*as long as she is otherwise unoccupied.* It is only when her energy is directed to outlets other than elaborate consumption or conspicuous waste, other than "Society," that her desire to keep servants will flag and her interest in domestic labour-saving machinery or arrangement will grow.

long as they can.   In support of the servant-keeping custom women are diligent too in arguments. Girls are much better off in domestic service, they allege, than in shops or factories.   "You can bring up children better in a private house than in an apartment."   There is more elegance in living in your own house than in an apartment; "it is cheaper too."—Indeed many women cling to keeping servants as the slaveholders of the South clung to keeping slaves.   In either case, the reasons by and large for this conservatism are hardly economic.   Are they not fundamentally psychological, keeping servants or slaves being not only a source of prestige, but supplying endless opportunities for ordering people about?

# WAGE EARNERS

O N the same day, one Henry Craydon, capitalist and factory owner, is asked by one man
to be kept on in a seasonal job and by another man to
be given a vacation from a permanent job. Both
men while working earn the same wage, $3.00 a day.
The first man is a factory hand who can not afford
to be laid off; the holiday-seeker is Mr. Craydon's
butler. "Look here," says Mr. Craydon, "how
do you account for it? One of my men from the
factory was here just now complaining that he
didn't have enough to live on. James, why is it
that he is a failure and you are a success?"

The butler smiled.

"Well, it's this way," he replied. "You see,
sir, I'm only a servant, but he, sir, is a Free and
Independent American Citizen."[1]

It is because he or she does not wish to be "only

[1] Masson, T. L., "An Easy Solution," *The New Republic*,
May 6, 1916.

a servant," the native-born American is reluctant, we often hear, to go into domestic service. Rather than be stigmatised by caste restrictions the American would forego a larger measure of economic comfort and stability. Quite similar sacrifices and for similar reasons are made sometimes by the salary earner who eschews manual or artisan labour, or even by the independent business man who eschews clerical or salaried positions.

Economic caste distinctions are gratifying to most of us. Through them we enjoy a sense of superiority. Nor do we limit the sphere of the distinctions to production. Through consumption a still greater measure of difference is achieved. This achievement is particularly characteristic of course in the class that can best afford to elaborate its consumption, the capitalist class, but within the labour class too different standards of living, *i. e.* of consuming make for caste demarcations. Cheap living is not accounted derogatory merely as a factor in lowering wages. To prove your worth or your husband's, whether you are in the labour class or the capitalist class, you must have things just as *good* as your neighbour, to keep your social position you must spend as freely. Conspicuous consumption, conspicuous waste is in all classes a manifestation of the will to power.[1]

It is a manifestation the upper classes would sometimes deny the lower. Witness upper class sumptuary legislation. During the sixteenth century, for example, French women were jailed by scores for wearing clothes above their station in life. At an earlier period the length of shoe points was determined by social position.[2] In colonial Massachusetts servants were forbidden to wear apparel too good for them, *i. e.*, exceeding the quality and condition of their persons or estates, under penalty of admonition for the first offence, a fine of twenty shillings for the second, and forty shillings for the third offence.[3]

[1] In his discussion of this feature in the leisure class Veblen rather under-emphasised its presence in the other classes. Analogously he underestimated it as a positive factor among leisure class women. Unending shopping and elaborate living are outlets for feminine energy as well as gratifications of masculine ambition. From this point of view many of the facts of that gynocratic caste we call American "Society" are to be interpreted. (See Parsons, E. C., *American "Society,"* an address published by the Chicago City Club.)

[2] Parsons, E. C., *Fear and Conventionality*, p. 64. New York, 1914.

[3] Salmon, p. 47.

Such legislation did not lessen the American's dislike of dressing in accordance with an economic status. Against liveries American "help" have always objected. Mr. Craydon's butler wore no doubt much more comfortable and certainly more expensive garments than Mr. Craydon's factory hand, but the labourer had the satisfaction of feeling that he wore what he liked, however illusory that feeling may have been. The labourer had also the satisfaction of feeling that he was master of his time—perhaps another illusion. "At any rate when I am not working my time is my own," is a very common argument for preferring factory to housework.

In labour circles the desire for personal independence expresses itself concretely in terms of time and pay. Owing to the exigencies of the wage system the expression, however, is indirect. The fight for the minimum day is not merely a fight for more leisure. The independent business man and the professional man do not strive for leisure. Their desire for leisure is curiously slight. The trade unionist's fight is not for leisure time, but for more time for himself. It is a never ending fight, for theoretically the worker can hardly be content until all his time is his own, *i. e.*, until he is his own employer. Similarly the fight for the minimum wage or for higher wages is a never ending fight, for mere increase of pay is not the fundamental issue. The fundamental and logical[1] issue is the elimination of the distinction between wage-earner and capitalist.

That the struggle over shortening the hours of labour or increasing its wage is not the ultimate struggle is most apparent in the open-shop issue. The employer is willing enough generally speaking to grant union conditions if he is allowed to feel he is granting them of his own accord, if he does not have to "recognise" the union, if he can hire or discharge his men at pleasure, if he can employ non-union as well as union men. "I'd rather go out of business," he asseverates, "than not be able to run my own business." It is his own sense of mastery he is defending.[2]   He is fighting for his

---

[1] Actually no doubt to most labour men the question of higher wages is only a business question, a matter of gain or profit.

[2] Employers "dislike the union because it challenges their supremacy. And they fight unions as monarchs fight constitutions, as aristocracies fight the vote. . . .   The labour problem, then, is at bottom the effort of wage-earners to achieve power." (Lippmann, Walter, *Drift and Mastery*, pp. 76, 94.   New York, 1914.)

status, for economic rule, and the fight is indeed closer to his heart than any fight for economic profits.

Let the employer but feel assured of his economic control and he may do a great deal to improve the condition of his employees—even over and above what he believes will add to their economic efficiency. He will give them libraries and schools and churches, build them model houses, plan in many ways for their health, their education, their comfort, in short he will be a model employer. All such uplift or social welfare enterprise contributes to his sense of power. To the more modern employer improving his work-people is more gratifying than economically enslaving or exploiting them. Like other social rulers he is inspired by the will to reform.

Sometimes he is surprised that his efforts do not meet with gratitude. As the old-time exploiter expected fear, so the modern exploiter expects gratitude. According to the method of the exploitation, fear or gratitude is the appropriate response, the response expected, we note incidentally, not only from the worker, the slave, the

6

servant, from the wage-earner or the "poor," but
the response expected of all subjects. The charge
of ingratitude is as efficient a whip as the charge of
disloyalty.

However we feel about it, we have to take note
that the modern worker has little sense of loyalty
or gratitude or, to use another euphemism, little
sense of responsibility to his employer. In short
he is indifferent to the interests of his employer.
He is considering his own interests, his own desire
for economic emancipation and economic rule.
To these ends trade unionism has contributed in
practical ways. More philosophic contributions
are made by socialism and syndicalism.

If the sense of mastery over his time and over his
tools is the worker's concept of economic freedom,
the industrial democracy[1] we call State socialism

[1] It is along the line of industrial democracy, in labour questions,
as we know, that the democratic struggle is waged today. Constitutional government, a department, as Veblen has described
it in his *Theory of Business Enterprise*, of the business organisation, allows only two democratic questions to impinge upon
it—the enfranchisement of women and local self-government.
Even these questions our political democracy entertains re-
luctantly, willing to play one against the other. Refusing a
constitutional suffrage amendment it makes the question of enfranchisement one of home rule. As for the home rule question
itself, it is obscured by traditional, mystical boundary lines.

will not satisfy him. The sense of personal subjection is no doubt lessened by government employment just as it is lessened by corporation employment compared with domestic service. But State employees do not feel themselves free workers. Under State socialism their sense of independence would be increased but little. To-day syndicalism, and syndicalism only, promises complete economic freedom to industrial workers. Not until they own or appear to themselves to own the machinery they run, not until they work for themselves, or, as they say, their ideals, are people able fully to exercise their will in their work.[1]

Desire for an ampler satisfaction of this kind

---

Not even in city government are actual conditions considered by the groups properly concerned. The formation of units of self-government will be one of the great realist problems of the future —once the hold on men's minds of the present fictitious units is loosened.

[1] That syndicalised industries would engage in inter-craft struggles and in monopolistic ventures of many kinds, that under syndicalism new economic castes would arise, seems to me well within the range of possibilities. Cp. Wallas, Graham, *The Great Society*, pp. 307–9. New York, 1914. For the moment we need not dwell on such problematical restrictions on social freedom.

Nor are we concerned here with syndicalistic methods, the general strike, *sabotage,* etc., methods which may well be, as Lippmann suggests, a grasping after industrial power characteristic of industrial impotence.

has begun to express itself in this country not only among industrial workers, but among producers of non-material values. There are signs of revolt against the capitalist, or rather against the business man, in both the learned and the artistic professions. Authors, actors, musicians, and teachers have taken up with the principles of unionism. Even university faculties are rebelling against the domination of trustees and trustee representatives. As for the professions of divinity, law, politics, medicine, and architecture they are still comparatively acquiescent; perhaps they are still satisfied with the remnants of social esteem they preserve from an older culture, perhaps they are satisfied with the share business allows them for their services to it, perhaps under their several codes of professional ethics they feel adequately unionised.

In course of time, however, the more content and conservative professions may also raise claims for more recognition from business; together with the present-day protestants, together with the most radical of industrial workers, they may even become syndicalised. Physicians may insist on owning their hospitals, college faculties on owning their universities, the clergy on owning their churches. But will the day ever come when all workers will conceive of freedom not through a reapportionment or reintegration of ownership but through that disappearance of ownership economists suggest as the logical conclusion of the machine process? So slight are the indications today either in practice or in theory of the imminence of this outcome, that it is difficult to speculate upon what in such an event would become the characteristic expressions of the "desire for power after power."

# "BACKWARD" PEOPLES

IT is a matter of general observation that until American immigrants learn the language or dialect and adopt the ways of the country—ways of dressing, of eating, of dwelling, of behaviour in general—they are subject to derision and contempt. As workmen they are especially exploited; even their fellow-workmen, native Americans, are prone to discriminate against them. Their children are teased or tormented, their wives ignored. As Micks, Dutchmen, Dagos, Sheenies, Waps, Hunkies, in innumerable ways they are made to feel their inferiority to the native born or to the naturalised citizen.

Naturalisation, as it is called in political terms, or, more comprehensively, assimilation is a complex process of classification which has of course more than one end. In this connection we have only to note that the process is also an end in itself. Making citizens is an outlet for the energy of

many groups of the native born.[1] When the
outlet is denied them, when foreigners are considered too disparate for assimilation to become
possible or when immigrants have resisted assimilation *en masse* by living in segregated communities,
the native born are gravely concerned.[2] They
feel thwarted and they look for relief. Restriction
of immigration is one of their favourite self-relief
measures.[3]

Recent world events have led to a notable outburst of the will to group solidarity in this country.
Many Americans seem to be taking the position of
the Law of the Twelve Tables where enemy and

[1] It is because native-born Americans so greatly value this outlet that they are prone to "believe in the miracle of the melting-
pot, which, like Medea's magic cauldron, will burn the old and
decrepit races of Europe into a young and vigorous people, newborn in soul and body. No other nation," adds the exception-
ally dismayed native born American I am quoting, "no other
nation cherishes this illusion." (Repplier, p. 202.)

[2] Note for example how the fact that in New Britain, Connecticut, the foreign population is nine times greater than the native
population seems to Miss Repplier "a hideous thing to contemplate." As autobiography of the "modest" American Miss
Repplier's chapter on "The Modest Immigrant" is unsurpassed.

[3] The pending Burnett immigration bill is a remarkable denial
of the right of international intercourse. It excludes from
admission into the United States Hindus and persons not eligible
for naturalisation (unless otherwise provided for by treaty, etc.).
It also extends certain privileges to immigrants who declare their
intention to become citizens.

alien were designated by the same term—*hostis*.
Ferocious attacks have been made on the hyphenated American or the immigrant who confesses to
any interest in the country of his birth. If one
can not serve two masters or two gods still less can
one sympathise with two nations. To be a good
American, the foreign born is told, he must not only
have no divided allegiance, he must forget he was
foreign born. At any rate in certain circles he may
not mention it. This campaign against hyphenated
and disloyal Americans is an outcome of a particular state of panic, to be sure, but it must also be
viewed as a consistent, if acute, part of the ordinary
American attitude towards the immigrant.[1]

[1] Or, to speak more justly, of the articulate Anglo-Saxon
American's attitude. As Horace M. Kallen has so clearly pointed
out, the Americanization problem is becoming not so much a
clash between native born and foreign born as between the
dominant economic class representing Anglo-Saxon culture and
the subordinate economic classes representing other European
cultures. Assuming with Miss Repplier and Mr. Kallen that
the melting-pot process must fail, are we headed with Miss
Repplier for "a caste system based on ethnic diversity" or with
Mr. Kallen for "a true federal state, such a state as men hope
for as the outcome of the European war, a great republic con-
sisting of a federation or commonwealth of nationalities"?
("Democracy Versus the Melting-Pot," *The Nation*, Feb.
18 and 25, 1915). For an admirable expression of the latter
political theory see Bourne, Randolph S., "Trans-national
America," *Atlantic Monthly*, July, 1916.

Americanisation is justified or extolled as a rule because of the higher standards of living held to be characteristic of the United States, and in these standards are included moral as well as economic levels. Immigrants are believed to be inferior because they come from inferior countries, from the effete or decadent civilisations of Europe, from races "old and decrepit," or from the savagery or barbarism of Africa or Asia. The existence of these American beliefs about the rest of the world is not due as much to scholastic ignorance, to gaps in the school curriculum, as to the social comfort brought by such beliefs. They form the fortifications, at large, of group conceit and self-assurance. Besides they help reduce all problems of immigration to the comparatively simple process of assimilation.

Zeal for raising the standard of living of "backward" peoples is not limited to those in our midst, it extends to those beyond our borders. Irrespective of their habitat we would better the economic and spiritual condition of any people lacking the privileges of American civilisation. We would have them live as we do, dress and eat like us, work and do business like us, have the same attitude towards property, the same sense of "law and order," have the same mating and family system, the same form of government, the same religion.

In these remoter fields the missionary has ever been the pioneer *par excellence.* To the prose-lytising religionist foreign groups can not fail to be alluring, for *ex hypothesi* the heathen may be classified in bulk as souls to be won. In fields unvisited of missionary it may be safely assumed that not a single native has been baptised or taken into the church. The magically redeeming words of the gospel none has heard. All are ripe for a spiritual harvesting. When a tribe comes to be baptised *en masse* the sense of achievement must be highly gratifying to their missionary.

But the missionary's opportunities for rule are by no means limited to religious conversion, to establishing ceremonial or enlarging the native pantheon. All the habits or customs of the natives in so far as they differ from his own habits or customs offer him opportunities. He, like others, finds differences immoral or degraded. To do

away with them therefore becomes his pleasing
duty. Armed with the commonplace social weap-
ons of ridicule, contempt, or fear, the missionary
undertakes to change the native dress or undress,
the native diet or drink, native dwellings—in short
to *improve* the material manner of living. Native
morals the missionary of course attends to—native
courtship and marriage, native infant and adoles-
cent practices, native mortuary practices. In
fact there is seldom anything[1] about native life
the missionary feels he cannot elevate. Missionaries have even been known to assert that a flexed
burial position, a "huddled up attitude," was
a "sign of degradation in the poor heathen."[2]
I find the Rev. Justus Doolittle arguing that the
Chinese need "the pure and elevating truths of
Christianity" because among other failures in

---

[1] I note one interesting exception in the recommendation of the
Rev. Justus Doolittle and the Board of Foreign Missions of the
Presbyterian Church not to teach Chinese converts English.
"The Chinese youth who have been taught English by mission-
aries have soon gone out of their control"—into secular pursuits.
(*Social Life of the Chinese*, II., 403, 404 ft. New York, 1865.) Cp.
Parsons, *The Old Fashioned Woman*, p. 283, on not teaching girls
and women foreign languages. Cp., too, the attitude of American
Church and State towards teaching negro slaves to read and
write.

[2] Routledge, p. 171.

theology they "have never been able to treat with distinctness the doctrine of the Creation," many of them regarding "the Bible account of the creation of the universe as only one of the various theories by which the origin of all things may be explained, and as by no means more reasonable than the theories which are current among themselves, or found in their ancient books."[1]

If the missionary gets a foothold at all, *i.e.*, if he is not killed at the start, he is likely to have some degree of prestige with the natives. This in itself is gratifying; then the feeling that he is spreading civilisation as well as religion must be intensely gratifying—to one who has no doubts about civilisation. To be the only representative of a culture in which you have full faith and to have opportunities, however limited, to establish it, must undoubtedly give one a sense of power. Even the denial of opportunities through native blindness or stiff-neckedness may give one a sense of superiority, a sense of itself flattering to the socially ambitious.[2]

[1] *Social Life of the Chinese*, II., 395, 396. Alack for such pre-Darwin Darwinians!

[2] The Rev. Doolittle points out what temptation there is for the *native* Chinese missionary to feel superior. Put forward "as

This particular shade of group conceit is not limited to the missionary in the field. It is felt by his supporters at home, felt not only by boards of foreign missions, but felt even more strongly perhaps by the ladies of the church missionary society. To do good vicariously to the poor heathen appeals to that particular maternal sense which expresses itself in improving the helpless. If members of missionary organisations feel they can save souls, feel, for example, that they can save the Chinese from dropping "into idolatrous graves at the rate of one for every third second," or, by another calculation, at the rate of 30,000 *per diem*, the satisfaction they get from praying or mite-giving can not be insignificant.

Such vicariousness in missionary zeal as well as the comprehensive efforts of the missionary in the field seem characteristic of Protestant mission work. Catholic or Buddhist missionaries have

teachers of their countrymen, pointing out their vices, their superstitions, and their idolatries, reproving them for these things . . . this position naturally begets a feeling of self-importance and superiority, especially as there is nothing in social life in China similar to the position they occupy. They are a new and distinct class, so to speak, which has certain peculiar privileges—those which belong to reformers and exhorters everywhere." (*Social Life of the Chinese*, II., 413–14.)

more or less confined their labours to ritualistic or spiritual enterprise, material and purely ethical conditions they. would not try to change. Their ambition seems to be satisfied by more restricted enterprises; perhaps their group conceit has been less than that of Protestants in progressive, modern nations. At any rate they have been satisfied with winning souls to God, to the Church, or to the Path.

But even these more moderate ambitions require a background of group conceit or self-assurance. Without it the stranger is too much feared to be a subject for conversion. Why add to his powers, the mystic powers that are very often imputed to him, by lending him your own supernatural aids and protectors? Primitive culture is too fearful to proselyte. It is religiously exclusive, secretive. Its ceremonials and myths are sacred chattels, so to speak, matters for a strict proprietorship. Their possession gives power and prestige, so why share? At any rate why should your own ancestral gods and the gods of your mountains and rivers, of your crops and herds, why should they go out of their way to take an interest in foreigners

—except to help you subjugate them? Your gods
are your serfs; home is the place for them.

The aspect changes if you plan not to leave
stranger peoples alone, but to conquer or to
exploit them. Then they must give allegiance to
your gods as well as to you. The more they
magnify your gods, the more they magnify you.
The more amenable they are to your gods, the
more amenable they are to you. So much em-
phasis has been placed in fact on this form of subservience that conquered groups who have resisted
"conversion" have been put to death. Believe
or die, the Moslem conquerer has insisted, and,
in many periods, the Christian. In India both
Moslems and Christians are said to have bought
slaves in order to proselytise them.[1] Slavery or
death is better than living in a state of sin—better
for the unregenerate, better for their benefactors.
The argument is unusually plainly stated, I find, in
a letter from Emanuel Downing to John Winthrop.
"A warr with the Narraganset is verie considerable
to this plantation," he writes in 1645, "ffor I
doubt whither yt be not synne in us, hauing power

[1] Thurston, p. 450.

in our hands, to suffer them to maynteyne the worship of the devill which theire paw wawes often doe; 2 lie, If vpon a Just warre the Lord should deliuer them into our hands, wee might easily haue men women and children enough to exchange for Moores, which wilbe more gaynefull pilladge for vs than wee conceive, for I doe not see how wee can thrive vntill wee gett a stock of slaves sufficient to doe all our buisines."[1]

Conversion by the sword, religious conversion, has ceased in Christendom, probably because of a growing indifference to religion, but the conversion of men's minds at large, as an Englishman has phrased it,[2] has not ceased, nor to this end has the sword wholly passed into disuse. Whether the pressure has been applied militaristically, economically, or otherwise, solicitude over "backward" peoples has been referred to in England as carrying the White Man's burden. The American equivalent is educating a people to order and self-government,[3]

[1] Salmon, p. 50 n. 1.

[2] "To give all men within its bounds an English mind—that has been the purpose of our empire." (Cramb, J. A., *Germany and England*, p. 141. New York, 1914.)

[3] Or, the slogan is making its *début*, to economic development or efficiency. In this connection Lippmann's suggestion to

the German equivalent is spreading *kultur*. For many years we Americans satisfied our will to power along this line among the "backward" peoples who voluntarily joined us, our immigrants; then we sought satisfaction, more or less fortuitously, in the West Indies and in the Philippines, among peoples whose consent to be governed was not always manifest. Recently we have shown a tendency to seek deliberately the same satisfaction in a country violently opposed

---

democratise the economic exploitation of "backward" peoples is of peculiar significance. He would stimulate popular interest in developing "backward" peoples by giving even the working class an economic stake in their exploitation. (*The Stakes of Diplomacy*, pp. 187–8. New York, 1915.)

The demand of the English liberal for a democratisation of diplomacy at large seems to be based on an analogous plan to share with all nationals satisfaction of the will to power over the foreign group.

From the humanist point of view diplomacy would profit little from democratisation, it seems to me, given existent groups. The democratic will over the foreign group might be almost as domineering or self-seeking as the will of a governing class or dynasty. The problem is not to distribute more equally predatory opportunities; it is the problem of regrouping populations, and of giving the new groups powers corresponding to their actual interests and responsibilities. (See *Social Freedom*, pp. 65 ff.) Lippmann's proposal for local international government for the world's undeveloped groups is acceptable enough from the point of view of national government. It does away with the pretentious fictions of imperialism. But what chance of self-government does it afford the "backward" peoples?

to gratifying us, in Mexico. As for the Germans, having no disorderly neighbour at hand and checked too in seeking to satisfy themselves through colonial dominion, they had of necessity to direct their energy in spreading *kultur* against the "backward" peoples of non-teutonised Europe.[1]

[1] The outcome of civilising activity is often unexpected. In Europe German ambition to civilise appears to have been frustrated, but in the United States it has met with an amazing success. In less than two years, Americans have been converted to a belief in a militaristic system that promises to out-Prussian Prussianism. New York State, for example, has decided to give military training to boys of sixteen. In Germany military training does not begin until the age of twenty.

The will to assimilate the immigrant or to exclude him has also been greatly stimulated throughout the United States by the European War. This points to further American conquest by the German spirit, *i. e.*, to a more ardent adoption in the United States of the German belief in nationalism.

# DELINQUENTS AND DEFECTIVES

THERE are many varieties of social rebels or delinquents and many have been the ways of disciplining them; the range of criminology even from the single point of view of the will to power in the law-abiding, the scope of penology thus limited is too great to undertake in this discussion. We should have to consider the punishments meted out to men-women or women-men, the unsexed, to the would-be old or would-be young, to the would-be learned or skilled, to the disobedient or impertinent or undignified in various positions of life, to the unchaste or adulterous, to the unfilial or unfaithful or disloyal, to the heretic or infidel or free thinker, to disturbers of the peace in other ways, to unauthorised poachers on the property or profession of others, to unauthorised mutilators or takers of life; we should have to consider punishment by ridicule, by degrading, by exile or ostracism, by pillory or chain or imprisonment, by fining or confiscating, by mutilating, raping, whipping, branding, and killing, by infection and disease, by enforced labour or enforced idleness, by miscellaneous forms of bodily and spiritual torture. Such a history of punishment should be written. It must suffice us for the moment, however, to consider some of the more general aspects of the treatment of delinquents.

In the view of crime we are taking, a deliberately one-sided view, the grievousness of the offence is gauged by the degree the will of the group or of the ruling class or classes has been thwarted or the degree to which the region the group or class arrogates to itself for its own expression has been trespassed upon. In other words, laws are in this sense but codifications of a group's will to power, codifications not to be tampered with either by subversion or by attempt at unauthorised execution. Duelling, for example, or the family or clan vendetta are accounted in modern culture improper interferences with the will of the larger inclusive group which has reserved the right to kill to itself. Contemporaneous world federationists would take even from the State part of this right, depriving single nations of the right to make war.

Whether the thwarting of the group or class will comes from without the group or class or from within, fear and the desire for reprisal[1] or vengeance are the feelings the check or encroachment arouse. By these feelings the treatment of delinquents has for the most part been determined or influenced. These feelings arouse the desire to get rid of criminals, to put them out of sight, to shut them off from fellowship. Imprisonment,

[1] The desire for reprisal seems greater when the offence is committed by an outsider or by an inferior. In proportion to crimes committed more negroes than whites are lynched by a community in which whites rule. It is probable that by a jury made up of employers of labour a labouring man would be pronounced guilty in a higher degree than he would be by a true jury of his peers, *i. e.*, by a jury of labourers. Among the Wataveta if a seducer belongs to the "age" of the husband he goes unpunished, if to the next "age," he is fined a goat, if to the "age" once removed, an ox. (Hollis, p. 124.) For theft in tenth-century England a free woman was thrown down a precipice or drowned, a woman slave was burned alive. (Pike, L. O., *A History of Crime in England*, I., 51. London, 1873.) For many centuries women, deprived of the benefit of clergy, could be executed for crimes for which men were only burned in the hand and for a short period imprisoned. For the murder of a spouse burning at the stake was the penalty for women, but not for men. An erring nun was taught to make "a candid confession" in these words: "Sir, I am a woman . . . therefore my sin is greater than if a man had done it, for it became me worse." (*The Ancren Riwle*, p. 317, Pub. Camden Society, 57. London, 1853.)

in particular solitary confinement, deprivation of
the rights of a citizen, and capital punishment are
the present-day penal policies, policies as much
due to fear and vengeance as was the hanging of
witches by New England Puritans or by Pueblo
Indians, as is the exiling of Russian revolutionaries to Siberia, as was in the ancient Roman
fashion sewing up parricides in leathern sacks
with a dog, a cock, a viper, and an ape and thus
setting them adrift.

Viewing imprisoned delinquents as a particularly helpless class, it is of great interest to note
to what lengths a modern community will go.
Prison regulations are aimed to break the convict's
spirit, subduing that individual wilfulness the
community resents. To this end methods of
deindividualisation are logical. The convict is cut
off from his friends, his family, and all intercourse
with the other sex. A rule of silence with fellow-
prisoners is imposed on him. He loses his name,
his choice of occupation, and all opportunities to
satisfy personal tastes. His hair is cut like his
fellows, he wears a uniform. He eats the same
food and keeps the same hours of sleep, exercise,

or work. In other words he is depersonalised by being strictly classified. Having convicted a man of unwillingness to accept one or more of its categories, society gets back at him by putting him in the most rigid category it can contrive—short of killing him or deifying him.

But some of the aforesaid prison methods are becoming antiquated. Solitary confinement is less resorted to, in many prisons a prison uniform has been discarded. Paying prison labour has been advocated—even in a national party platform. Attempts to establish more normal social relations in general between the prisoners and between prisoners and their keepers are under way. A desire to reform is succeeding the desire for reprisal. We may expect to see this impulse to reform prisoners instead of punishing them gain considerable headway in the future, providing the law-abiding classes are assured that they are as well—if not better—protected against criminals by the new prison methods as by the old. Under such circumstances the collective will to power may be as much gratified by reforming men as by torturing them. Indeed, once the factor of fear is eliminated, improving others may be even more gratifying than destroying them.[1] I doubt if even the public hangings once so enjoyed in England afforded as much satisfaction to managers and onlookers as a meeting I recently attended in behalf of New York State prison reform. The audience of three or four thousand persons had an opportunity to express their support of a public official persecuted, they held, because of his prison reforms. That expression of opinion was in itself gratifying, but the exhibit on the platform of ex-convicts, men redeemed to society by the new prison methods, was still more gratifying. Here were men made over, men become willing members of the group they had defied and attempted to thwart. Their promise henceforward "to go straight," *i. e.*, as the law-abiding willed, probably gave that law-abiding audience a greater sense of

[1] The elements of submission and improvement are what make the spectacle of penance so pleasing, not the element of punishment. Supporting a Magdalen Asylum or home for fallen women is a source of deeper gratification, I surmise, than fining or segregating or marking prostitutes, just as sending a man on a pilgrimage to Rome or Jerusalem or prescribing a fast or a hair shirt must have been more gratifying than locking him up or disfiguring him. · The Church, after all, and not the State, has ever been the past master of the art of gratifying the will to power.

achievement than passing any sentence to torture or imprisonment or than condemning those ex-convicts to further social ostracism, sacrificing them to the usual inclination not to be bothered by men with a criminal record.[1]

The old-time classification of ex-convicts and convicts is being challenged not alone by the penologist. Eugenist and alienist have begun to take delinquents out of their customary categories —to put them into new. Nowadays delinquents are coming to be considered and treated more and more as defectives. Other considerations aside, the theory of crime as disease or unsoundness is the more acceptable because it lends itself to the growing desire to reform rather than penalise.

Reform schools are interesting places, I have found, to study the relation between these two expressions of the will to power. How close the

[1] It is this general inclination which makes the comparative leniency of modern penal laws more or less nominal. "When the law does not rid us of you for ever," say the law-abiding to the ex-convict, "we shall do it for ourselves. We at least refuse to re-classify you. Once a prisoner always a prisoner, for there are other than prison walls. Branding for life may have passed as a penal fashion, but there is another form of stigmatising, a psychical or social stigmatism, still at our disposal."—This attitude is a form of contempt of court which goes as yet unpenalised.

relation may be, how easy the transition, I realised not long since on a visit to a girls' reform school in Pennsylvania. Here the "incorrigibles" were tested periodically for feeble-mindedness and the object of the testing had not been concealed from the tested girls. A mental test so understood would seem to approximate cellular confinement or any other method of letting a prisoner know his place.[1]

Just as today there may not be much difference in treatment whether the delinquent is classed as a delinquent or whether he is classed as a defective, so formerly, however the defective was classed, he was treated as a delinquent. Maniacs were killed, in England commonly by fire, or, let live, they were chained to a post under a shed or in the open. Believed to be possessed of an evil spirit, they were beaten by passers-by anxious to do God a service. Even after asylums were established, the mode of life for the insane was of a more or less

---

[1] Women as a sex have been shown their place by similar methods. Within recent years, for example, Dr. Möbius, a German physician of some ability, published a book on the "physiological weak-mindedness of women." (Ellis, Havelock, *The Task of Social Hygiene*, p. 91. Boston and New York, 1912.)

penal character, with half rations, the dark cell, the strait-jacket, and flagellation, the common methods of control.    In China flagellation is a way of disciplining lepers.    Lepers are assembled in an asylum under a head man.    The rules are very rigid and if an inmate break them, the head man may with impunity beat him to death. [1]    In France until the fourteenth century a man pronounced a leper was ceremonially killed.    He was taken to the church and a burial service held over him. His heirs took all his property and his wife was free to marry again.    "As to your little wants," the priest said to him as he thrust him from the church door, "good people will provide for them, and God will not desert you." [2]

Sequestration, torture, death have been the lot of defectives in all communities.    They may be killed at birth or, when the abnormality is not or does not appear congenital, in later years.    Where social standards are opposed to killing the abnormal, as in general in Christendom, the aversion may express itself in sentimental attitudes result-

[1] Doolittle, II., 254.
[2] Michelet, J., *Histoire de France*, IV., 140.    Paris, 1879.

ing in derision or neglect.    The treatment of deaf-mutes is an illustration.    Until the close of the eighteenth century, if not later, deaf-mutes were accounted sinful creatures, their affliction a visitation of Providence, and no effort was made to put them into systematic communication with their fellows.    About the middle of the eighteenth century the Abbé de l'Epée worked out a finger code of communication for the deaf and began to teach them writing.    That this simple plan was not invented long before is a striking illustration of the effect of the lack of social pressure upon inventiveness, also of the kind of social inhibition theories of the "hand of God" may favour.    The delay in inventing an alphabet for the blind is a like twofold illustration.

The service of God also has been a burden upon defectives.    To it the mentally defective have often been devoted.    Court servitude has been the lot of the deformed in body in many societies. Under the Roman Emperors dwarfs were compelled to fight in the gladiatorial shows.[1]    In the

[1] Lecky, I., 298.    Maimed and feeble men were also compelled to fight.    There were also women gladiators.    The opposition to

courts of the Renaissance dwarfs were mated to propagate their abnormality and their offspring served as gifts of prince to prince. In many communities the mating of the defective has been especially regulated. Today in our own culture eugenists are prescribing for defectives sterilisation or segregation during the reproductive period.

---

patricians going into the ring is significant of the servile character imputed to the gladiatorial contest. The same servile character attaches not uncommonly to actors. May it be that the drama gratifies, as did the gladiatorial contest, the will to power of the audience, the onlooker seeing in the player a servant of his desires, one to show life as he, the onlooker, would have it, to represent characters the onlooker would like either to assume or to dismay or worst. Here is a clue—not a novel clue—to the enjoyment at least of melodrama. It is an explanation too of why the drama is able to oust from popularity sports like bull or bear baiting as it did, for example, in England in the seventeenth century. Psychologically the theory offers a clue, too, to the not uncommon exclusion of children and of women from playgoing. In the religious origin of the drama there is of course another, if not entirely-unrelated, explanation of this exclusion.

Is it a mere coincidence that during the past half century when the stage has become serious, *i. e.*, arrogated moral and educational functions, women and children have been more freely allowed to go to the play and the profession itself has become more respected? As actors turn preachers they become ruling-class.

# THE "LOWER" ANIMALS

THE Platonic theory of punishment after death was reincarnation first in a woman and then, that form of torture ineffectual, in the animal the bad ghost resembled.[1] Hindu theories of retribution are similar. A thief of grain becomes a rat; of honey, an insect; of meat, a vulture; of perfume, a muskrat; of fruit or roots, a monkey; of silk, a partridge; of linen, a frog. As for a disobedient wife, after death, Manu declares, she will enter the womb of a jackal.[2] Such classifications of the dead are not only an expression of the will to degrade; there is also, I surmise, the feeling that as one of the lower animals the reincarnated spirit will be quite subject to the rule he tried to escape as a human being.

In their rule over animals men have exemplified very freely the various phases of that will to power we have been considering—the destructive phase, the enslaving phase, and the supporting or

[1] *Timæus*, 42, 90.　　　[2] *Manu*, XII., 62-9; IX., 30.

protective phase. The history of hunting, fish-
ing, and trapping needs no particularisation. The
satisfactions afforded by those activities are of
course fuller in the cultures where fish or wild
animals are the mainstay of subsistence, but needless to say zest for the chase or for angling is found
under almost all economic conditions. Given natural opportunity, it has been curbed or thwarted
only by potent religious argument. The Chukchee
will not fire on a wolf because he believes a wolf is a
shaman incarnate.[1] A Blackfellow will not hurt a
crow or a wild dog because it is his totem, nor a
West Coast African, a python because the spirit of
an ancestor may be embodied in it. Thanks to their
more generalised theories of reincarnation Hindus
will not kill any animals or eat their flesh. To fulfil
a vow or give thinks to the gods the Chinese will
"let live" not only all kinds of domestic animals,
but wild birds, fish, eels, and turtles.[2] Such dedicated creatures are supported or "protected."

----

[1] Bogoras, Pt. I., pp. 81-2. But he will lasso a wolf at-
tacking reindeer.

[2] Doolittle, II., 181-2. I commend to the curious reader
Doolittle's account of Chinese vegetarianism and *ex-voto* animals.
It is an important contribution to the study of the animal pet.

This Chinese dedication of living creatures is obviously a twofold gratification; through it men work their will not only upon the sacrificial creature, but upon the divine recipient of the sacrifice. Animal blood-sacrifice is an analogous gratification. In magic as well as in religion animals may provide gratification in more than one way. There is for example the custom of the scapegoat, the selection of an animal to expiate or carry off sickness or sin. The Hebrews were not the only people to turn an animal out into the wilderness to suffer for them[1] and cleanse them of sin. When a Caffre of South Africa is ill a goat may be taken into his presence and the sins of the kraal confessed over it. After a few drops

[1] Vicarious suffering is exacted of other subject classes. When a Baganda army was threatened with evil on its return from war a woman captive together with a cow from the booty, a goat, a fowl, and a dog were sent back to the border where, their limbs broken, they were left to die. Tied to these victims were bunches of grass which had been rubbed over the Baganda to take away the potential disaster. In great emergencies the Rajah of Manipur and his wife would bathe on a scaffold and let the water drip from them upon a criminal crouched beneath. With the drippings their sins were washed away to the criminal. (Frazer, J. G., *The Golden Bough*, Pt. VI.; *The Scapegoat*, pp. 39, 42. London, 1913.) The theory of vicarious suffering plays an important rôle in Christianity, and by the doctrine of the atonement, if by nothing else, the Christian manifests his domineering attitude towards deity.

of the invalid's blood are let fall upon the goat's
head the animal will be turned out into the desert
to carry with it the people's troubles.   Similarly
in Arabia in time of pestilence a camel will be led
through a town to take on itself the evil and then
to be strangled.   Formosans drive the demon of
small-pox into a sow and then cut off the animal's
ears and burn them or it, thus ridding themselves
of the plague.[1]   In these ritualistic performances
we see exemplified, I repeat, what we may call the
principle of twofold or multiple gratification; a
subject creature in this case is mutilated or killed
or driven away or cast off—casting off is always
an arrogation of power[2]—and people at 'the same
time purify themselves, turn over a new leaf, an
act which gives a sense of self-control.

The scapegoat is a collectivist assertion.   Of

[1] *The Scapegoat*, pp. 31–33.
[2] This assertive act of casting-off or exiling takes place in connection with most of the subject classes—offspring are disin-
herited or driven out of the family, a flagrant instance of the
reassertion of a parental will which has been thwarted, wives in
quite similar case are repudiated or divorced, servants too are
dismissed, wage-earners are locked out, criminals are banished
from tribe or nation, kings and revolutionaries are exiled, Hell
is a place of exile for the dead, and its chief, disobedient to the
will of God, is himself an exile from Heaven.   For the banishment of other spirits see pp. 141, 142.

8

the fact that maltreatment of animals, their abus-
ive killing or maiming, is also a sporadic and
individualistic indulgence, due for the most part
perhaps to a thwarted will, any society for the
prevention of cruelty to animals has records.
Instances have been noted too among peoples
where no such societies are organised.[1] Bogoras
relates that a certain Chukchee reindeer herder was
on one occasion so teased by the unruliness of his
reindeer-herd that he stopped running after the
animals and, turning ceremonially to the setting
sun, invited the wolves to come and devour the
herd. "Here wolves, catch them and eat them,"
he called out. "That time I spoke foolishly,"
commented the man in telling the story, "because
I felt my weakness. When I was younger, I could
assuage my anger [when the herd scattered] by
outrunning the reindeer."[2]

The well known cruelty of children to animals
which is ascribed as a rule to their lack of imagina-

[1] Sometimes a supernatural sanction takes the place of a S. P.
C. A. The Chukchee are said not to strike their draft reindeer
very hard. Maltreatment of reindeer or dogs is considered a
great sin against Life-giving-Being. (Bogoras, p. 89.)

[2] *The Chukchee*, pp. 46, 567.

tion, their inability to put themselves in the place
of the tortured creature, this infantile cruelty
must also be explained as a manifestation of an
imperious will. Into the desire to see what a
creature will do when it is pinched or squeezed or
teased or mutilated enters gratification from the
imperious act itself. Cruelty to animals, teasing
them, is one of the comparatively few outlets[1] open
to children to exercise their will. Taking care of
their bird or animal pets is the other aspect of their
control over inferior creatures.

Children are notably fond of pet animals. So
are women, particularly childless women. So
are unmarried men. "None as companionable as
a dog," declares the old bachelor. And none so
servile as the "servant of man," none so uncritical,
so little given to talking back—not even a well
trained wife. Not that married men and women
with children are not fond too—if to a less extent—
of pet animals. It was not unusual in New Zea-
land to see a Maori woman carrying her child at
her back and a pet dog or pig in her bosom. Baki-
ma men are said to love their cattle like children,

[1] Younger children and dolls afford other outlets.

to pet and coax them, talk to them, weep over their ailments, and "should a favourite die their grief is so extreme that it sometimes leads to suicide."[1]

Animal dependence brings with it, like other kinds of dependence, opportunities for doing things to the kept creatures—docking their tails,[2] making patterns in their coats by branding, shaving, etc., dressing them up as we dress up dogs or monkeys, naming them, "showing" them, racing them, breeding them, gelding them, suckling them as savage women have been known to suckle puppies or monkeys, making them fight as we have set cocks, dogs, badgers, or bulls against their own species or another, making them hunt[3] or, like

[1] Westermarck, II., 494, 496.

[2] The Chukchee crop the tails of their dogs as a punishment. Disobedient dogs will have their tails cropped on the road and will have to go on pulling till evening, the blood trickling all the while. (Bogoras, p. 103.)

[3] Realistically, like dogs or falcons or ferrets, or magically like the prey animals the Zuñi carry with them on their hunts in the form of little stone fetiches.

Of the enslavement of the spirit of a beast of prey, I find a many-sidedly instructive instance in the practice of the Kuki-Lushai of Assam. The killer of a tiger dresses himself up as a woman, lets down his hair, smokes a woman's pipe, and spins a cotton spindle. All this he does, it is alleged, to humble the ghost of the tiger by making him believe he has been shot by a woman. [Shakespear, J., in *Journal Anthropological Institute*, XXXIX. (1909), 380–1.]

the Japanese cormorant, catch fish, deifying them
like the sacred horse of Japan, the white elephant
of Siam, the ibis of Egypt, training them to perform all manner of tricks, teaching them to speak,
to count, to dance, to "beg," to "say please,"
in short to act like men. [1]—Where could one find,
by the way, a more vivid token, not only of professional mendicancy, [2] but of the attitude more or less
expected of every subject creature than in the picture
of a dog constrainedly erect on his haunches "saying
please" for the lump of sugar held above his nose?

For the enslavement of animals we turn of
course to the history of their domestication.   Like
prisoners of war, animals that could not be domesticated as a rule were killed; when they could be
broken in or tamed, again like captives of war, they

---

[1] See *The Island of Dr. Moreau* by H. G. Wells for a picture
of human energy venting itself unrestrained upon animals.   As
Circe and the transmigrationists would turn men into brutes, so
Dr. Moreau would turn brutes into men, change them physically.

[2] Although historically the disappearance of mendicancy is to be
accounted for by the disappearance of the practice of buying a
way to heaven, the disrepute of mendicancy being primarily the
discredit of a religious practice or function, yet the lapse of alms-
giving in general out of modern culture may also be taken, it
seems to me, as one of the signs that the gratification of feeling
superior is in process of being foregone—at least in regard to
certain classes.

were put to the service of the captors. But even the most serviceable animals, draft animals and animals for food, even animals kept for religious purposes, were domesticated, I surmise, not alone for utilitarian or religious reasons; their domestication gave of itself a sense of power.[1]

Here lies part of the explanation, let us note incidentally, why in so many herding communities the women are forbidden having anything to do with the herds. A Kikuyu woman may not even drink cow's milk, nor a Toda pass over the trail taken by the sacred buffalo or have anything to do with that part of the hut where the churning takes place.[2] Such restrictions are not due merely to an association of ideas, as is sometimes alleged, to

[1] The psychology of agriculture might be considered from the same point of view. The social attitude towards vegetal life shows the same phases as toward animal or human life—the destructive, the exploiting, the protective. Is it fanciful to see in my lady's flower garden and in the gentleman's estate correspondences with the pet animal, the spoiled child, and the kept woman? For a picture of non-proprietary cultivation one turns to Maurice Hewlitt's account of the man who made all England his garden.

To make things beautiful, not to get beautiful things for oneself, not even to express one's sense of beauty through medium as individualistic as paint or clay or verse, to add beauty to the world itself and to its creatures, some day this may be the rôle expected of the artist.

[2] Routledge, p. 45. Rivers, *The Todas*, pp. 27, 30.

the fact that herding as a derivative of hunting is conceived of as a male occupation. Herding as well as hunting favours that exercise of will with which interference from the weaker sex is not tolerated.

The creatures that resist domestication, various species of "wild" beasts and of birds, such unenslavable creatures, are imprisoned, caged, displayed in royal courts, in the circus, in zoölogical gardens. The plea that the prisoners of the "zoo" are merely held for popular instruction has become more tenable in recent years when their artificial habitat has been rendered as like their native habitat as circumstances permit; but even this bit of rationalism cannot be advanced for the confinement of creatures in a circus. As for the potentates who kept menageries, as for conquerors who included wild beasts in their "triumphs" or games, educational needs were far indeed from their minds. When Caesar marched up the Capitoline with forty torch-bearing elephants[1] on

[1] What was the function, one wonders, of the elephant that marched in a recent suffrage parade in Chicago and in the indoor parade of the delegates to the Republican National Convention? A means of educating the voters or a symbol of sex or party prowess?

his right and on his left, when Caligula had four
hundred bears killed in one of his gladiatorial
shows, these rulers were not engaged in educating
the Roman schoolboy, but in inspiring the Roman
populace with an appreciation of imperial prowess.
The foremost chief of the Kič, a tribe in Central
Africa, kept a cage from which thanks to his skill
in ventriloquism the roars of imaginary lions and
the howls of imaginary hyenas were heard to issue.
He gave out that these beasts guarded his house,
and were ready at his bidding to rush forth on his
enemies.  Another Central African chief kept a
real tame lion at his doorstep and four real snakes.[1]
The Obeah man of the West Indies works " witch "
through snakes and cats and I know a most estim-
able Bahaman commissioner who is not above
securing prestige among his islanders through
keeping a spotless black cat as a member of his
household.

[1] Frazer, J. G., *Lectures on the Early History of the Kingship*, pp.
115, 116.  London & New York, 1905.

# THE DEAD

A SICK animal is said to go off alone to die, and ailing creatures are sometimes killed by their fellows. Among human beings these attitudes are at times institutionally paralleled. The dying are put away—sometimes in shelters, sometimes in exposed places. Women in labour are often segregated. The decrepit are sometimes killed. So are the insane, as we have noted, or those born abnormal. Decrepitude, invalidism, pain, abnormality of any kind are trying to the sound and well and it is to ease themselves they get rid of the distasteful and depressing objects. Whatever the rationalistic explanations the normal and vigorous may make themselves, they banish or kill from the same feeling a child entertains when he begs to have his maimed pet, his dog or bird, disposed of—he "just can't bear the sight of it." He will cure his pet if he can, but if he can't, he would kill it. Cure or kill are the relief alternatives.

Killing is taken, however, only if curing fails. Apart from sympathetic impulses to cure, doctoring is gratifying in itself. It means control over several classes of persons—over the patient, over the patient's family or circle, over the human or spirit enemies of the patient, the evil beings responsible for his sickness. No wonder medicinemen or doctors are usually ruling-class.

Medicine-men belong to the governing classes logically and practically. Practically, however, there are periods where their social position suffers. These are periods when professional methods are changing, the new methods not having yet acquired the repute lost by the old. Modern medicine has been passing through just such a phase. As soon as the practice of medicine began to discard the esoteric ways of a more primitive art, it began to lose prestige; in the eighteenth and nineteenth centuries doctors appeared as self-revealed quacks. They had given their tricks away. Besides, in that period, in spite of differentiating themselves from supernaturalists, they suffered from the general decay of supernaturalism. Loss of faith in God meant loss of faith in those who were still remembered as his proxies.

Modern medicine has still to assert itself. When it is generally realised that the doctors are stamping out disease, fighting epidemics,—I use the phrases already significant of professional potency,—cleaning up whole quarters of the globe, lowering the mortality rate of vast populations, prolonging life, when this realisation sinks in, then the doctors will come into their own again. Meanwhile it is a curious situation that in this ambitious country there is as yet no federal department of public hygiene and that nation-wide campaigns against typhoid, syphilis, diphtheria, tuberculosis, poliomyelitis, are ungeneralled and inchoate. I incline to think that through their prosecution of epidemic-causing witches or through their raids against the tribes of medicine-men who have sent fatalities among them, peoples of primitive culture still get more sense of power over the causes of disease than the peoples of civilisation, indifferent to magic or religion and yet neglectful of the vast field of public hygiene science has opened to the exercise of power.

However influential and masterful the doctors may become in the near future as public health servants, as we say, or as arbiters even over the right to marry or to procreate, it is probable that power to shorten life will be withheld for long from the medical profession and limited as at present to the legal and military professions.    In societies where the functions of chieftancy are less differentiated than in modern society, the chiefly medicine-man may have power over the duration of life.    Such power is compatible with the unsophisticated desire to get rid of those fatally ill.

Although this desire is for the most part, as I say, mere reluctance to sympathise—it is too disturbing to see people die slowly—there is too in the treatment of the moribund a kind of impatience, a wish to hasten the end which may be fairly described as a wish to control death. The dying is speeded on his journey in much the same spirit a lingering guest may be given a present or bidden farewell to get rid of him.    The Zuñi put food into the mouth of the dying as sustenance, it is said, for the journey to Kothluwala. The South Sea Islanders Hocart tells of hung leaves over their dying kinsman to drive away the spirits who were holding him back from a similar journey.[1] On a recent visit to Andros Island in the Bahamas the prayer of an old negro acquaintance at the death-bed of his wife was repeated to me. "Good Lo,' take her out of her misery," he had begged. "Good Lo', hurry her up."

And as the guest who never knows when to go wears out his welcome so the moribund who recovers is not always cordially received back into society. The aged Hindu who returns home after the rite of immersion in the sacred river is disgraced the rest of his life. Bose knew one old widow who after returning home from repeated immersions drowned herself from shame.[2] There is a story from the Islands of the Torres Straits of an islander whose funeral rites had been performed, returning home. His people at first refuse to believe it is he and then, outraged at the idea of having gone through a funeral for a living man, they club him to death.[3]

[1] In Folk-Lore, XXVI. (1915), 132.

[2] The Hindoos as They Are, pp. 257 ft., 259. Calcutta, 1883.

[3] R. C. A. E. T. S., V., 90. For a parallel in English fiction see Parsons, E. C., "Ironies of Death," The New Republic, March 11, 1916.

Nor is the ghost suffered to linger—at least for long.  He may be given a specified time to "walk" in, to cling to his people and his possessions, but that time elapsed he is firmly bidden begone, he is sped on his journey to where the dead belong, he is exorcised.  And no end of measures are taken to keep him from returning, from haunting those who would have nothing of him but what they can themselves determine.  From having any wayward influence on them he is, if they can manage it, to be completely excluded.  They take precautions against dreaming of him or pining for him.  They fumigate themselves.  They wear something to make them forget.[1]  They will not allow the deceased to be named in their presence.[2]  Except in the ways the survivors appoint, a ghost is an exile from his old home.

[1] For example, the Hupa Indians of North California wear strands of grass around their neck to keep from dreaming of their dead.  (Goddard, p. 73.)

[2] In many communities naming the dead or even objects of the same name is a dire "insult" to survivors.  Unapologised for, *i. e.*, uncompensated, it will be avenged.  This custom, curious to us, is an illustration, I think, of the outlet that may be found by a thwarted purpose, in this case the purpose to put the dead out of mind.  The sense of insult is deserving of analysis.  Is it a recuperative device under circumstances of frustration, a means towards securing reparation or restoration of the sense of power?

This banishment does not mean that the survivors fail to care for the deceased. They provide him not only with comfort for his journey but with lasting resources, with food, drink, clothing, personal equipment, with favourite animals, even with slaves or wives.[1] Dying unmarried he may have a living bride bestowed upon him.[2] The Chinese even have "matchmakers for disembodied souls." In short a ghost is made well off in his new habitat, well off in goods and in prestige. All this his people do for him, and in view of the gratification it gives them, for them-

[1] From the point of view of the deceased, funeral sacrifice or immolation is a recognition of his will to power. Hence the greater the recognition in life, the greater will it be in death. As a rule, children, slaves, and women are sacrificed only to the chiefly class.

Sometimes a chieftain, like Mutesa of Uganda, for example, will ask *not* to have his women killed at his death, an act of "mercy" probably not entirely without gratification to him. Similarly a modern husband on his death-bed may express a wish that his expectant widow marry again.

Generally speaking testamentary bequest appears to substitute for funerary destruction, the last wishes of the deceased, the "dead hand," for a less personal mourning service.

Revolt against the "dead hand" may be interpreted as denial by the living of power to the dead. An inheritance tax is an analogous denial. So is the denial of testamentary disposition to self-murderers, a practice in England until 1870 and in force today in Russia.

[2] Parsons, *Religious Chastity*, pp. 56-7.

selves, and they may go on for years making the deceased presents. Even members of the church that once gave notice so firmly to the dead that having brought nothing into the world they were to take nothing out, even Christians burn candles to the dead and bring flowers to their graves.

But in return for these presents or for the initial funerary endowment, the living expect services from their dead, they ask for their aid in every conceivable way. When a Zuñi woman scatters a bit of food before her meal she says: "Take this and give us rain and make our child grow up strong." A Bageshu expects his ancestral ghosts to look after his marital honour. He expects the ancestor for whom he names a child to kill it should it be an illegitimate.[1] The Chinaman expects his deceased parent to multiply to him the money (it is only paper, make-believe money at that) placed in his coffin.—Indeed the blessings of the dead are no mere figure of speech to those who believe their dead are really accessible.

And of unrelated as well as of related dead

[1] Roscoe, p. 184.

benefits are expected. Bits of the corpses of men of unusual valour or vigour may be eaten[1] to derive their virtues. Relics of heroes or saints are expected to work miracles of cure or generalised aid. We noted the enslavement of the ghosts of foreign enemies.

The living exact unending service of the dead, and, a point not always mentioned I think, unending dependence. The welfare of the dead is conditioned upon their cult. Any lapse on the part of the living is enough to make the dead unsettled, shabby, famished, miserable. Were they not to dress the corpse properly, the Hupa believe, the ghost would look ill-arrayed for ever since it presents throughout all time the appearance of the corpse at burial.[2] In Bikol, Luzon,

[1] Aside from its utilitarian aspect cannibalism has been considered as an expression of sympathetic magic. It should also be considered as an act of power. To devour your enemy or your subject is gratifying. The gods are sometimes seen to get this satisfaction from human sacrifice, and men get it, I surmise, when they eat their gods or symbols of their gods. Prisoners of war are sometimes eaten and women captives have been known to have been married and then eaten. Wives are sometimes eaten in Australia, but here under circumstances of famine. In folk-tales, however, wives are eaten by way of reprisal. From the ogres who devour wayward and troublesome children I suspect parents of drawing a vicarious bit of satisfaction.

[2] Goddard, p. 71.

9

unless a corpse is beaten by the native priestesses[1] the deceased is subject to torture by an intrusive demon. By considering the bill of fare drawn up by the Hindu for deceased ancestors it may be seen how easily they may be starved. "Ancestors are satisfied for one month," says Manu, "with sesamum grains, rice, barley, water, roots, fruits, etc.; for two months with fish; three months with gazelle meat; four with mutton; five with birds' flesh; six with kids' flesh; seven with spotted deer; eight with black antelope; nine with Ruru deer; ten with boars and buffaloes; eleven with hares and tortoises; one year with cow-milk and milk-rice; twelve years with white goat."[2]

Nor in the theories of life after death, at least

---

[1] Frazer, *The Scapegoat*, p. 260. Whipping is a very ubiquitous display of power. Evil spirits are quite commonly beaten out of the possessed, so are ghosts out of mourners. Children, women, slaves, criminals, animals, all are subject to scourging. See the account of flogging sailors in Dana's *Two Years before the Mast*, as an unusually patent self-gratification through flagellation. "Don't call on Jesus Christ," shouted Captain Thompson. "He can't help you. Call on Frank Thompson! He's the man! He can help you! Jesus Christ can't help you now! . . . Now you know what I am! I'll make you toe the mark, every soul of you, or I'll flog you all, fore and aft, from the boy up! You've got a driver over you! Yes, a slave-driver,—a nigger-driver. I'll see who'll tell me he isn't a nigger slave!"

[2] *Laws*, III., 123.

in the continuation theories peculiar to early culture, are the dead suffered to make any changes for
themselves. They have to exist just as they have
always existed, a little better off perhaps, but
living in the same general style, confined to the
same circle of acquaintances or kinsfolk. Their
very age stays the same. As a rule the old
remain old, the young remain young. An old
woman, a New Yorker, once told me that as
she entered the gates of Heaven the first person
she expected to see was the little girl she had
lost a half century ago. "She will run out to
meet me just as she did then; she was just five
years old."

Not only the age-class of the dead remains static,
their sex and their habits are fixed. As a rule men
have to remain men, and women, women. There
are instances, however, when bad men are degraded
into women, and super-excellent women[1] pro-

[1] An eighteenth century traveller in China relates that the
priests of Fo promised women, in return for their favours, to
change their sex. "At present," said the priests, "you are the
weak and servile sex, . . . but when you are born again into
the world you shall become men." (Astley, Th., *Voyages and
Travels*, IV., 215. London, 1747.) See p. 155 for the Princess
Amva of Benares.

moted into men.[1] As for intimacy between deceased men and women, it may be denied them
altogether or in part. The Nahuatl relegated the
sexes to different heavens; it may be impossible
for Kuki'-Lashai women to get into Mi-thi-khua,
the dead men's village, because they are shot at
by its watchman, the ghost of the First Man[2];
Christians and certain Melanesians admit women
to heaven, but they taboo marriage there; the Zuñi
decree that wherever the affections of a much
married man or woman may lie, it is with his or
her *first* mate he or she must live in Kothluwala.

Even with these limitations upon their freedom
of action, the dead who merely go on living as they
lived before death may be supposed not to be
much interfered with by the living. That is the
conservative way the dead in all probability would
choose for themselves. Averse to change in life

[1] Parsons, *The Old-Fashioned Woman*, pp. 320-1. The Hakka
of China are said to put girls at times to a cruel death in order that
they may be reincarnated as boys. (Westermarck, I., 401.)

[2] Shakespear, p. 379.

At Saa, in the Solomon Islands, there are two classes of ghosts,
*lio'a*, ghosts of power, and *akalo*, ghosts of no account. Male
ghosts are classified according to their position in life, but no
female ghost can be a ghost of power. (Codrington, R. H., *The
Melanesians*, p. 262. Oxford, 1891.)

as are people of primitive culture, they would inferentially be averse to change after death. Such change were punishment.[1] It is not adequate punishment, however, where the retribution theory of life after death crops out. Then at least the living really begin to feel their power over the dead. They indulge in a very orgy of rewards and punishments, particularly punishments. The reward and punishment theory of after life has been one of the most effectual instruments of social control society has ever produced. It cuts so many different ways. It serves to control the living, very many classes of the living, all subject classes in fact except animals, it may even be worked against supernaturals, and it reduces the dead to utter subjection. The bad man who in earlier cultures becomes a bad spirit to annoy or distress the living, under the retribution theory is held fast and for ever in remote torturous regions. The Christian, the Buddhist, and the Gaina hells show

[1] A unique character was the old Yuchi Indian Speck describes as asking to be buried facing the west because, being a progressive man, as he said, disgusted with old conditions, he did not wish to travel towards the east, the path of his ancestors. ("Ethnology of the Yuchi Indians," p. 98, *Anthrop. Pub. Univ. Penn. Mus.*, I, Phila., 1909.)

to what amazing lengths the will to power may go. Even the comparatively good person, in the catholic system of Heaven, Purgatory, and Hell, is somewhat dependent on the living, for may not the living by their prayers and offerings shorten his journey from Purgatory to Heaven?

Today among us the doctrine, if not of Heaven, at least of Hell is losing its serviceability. Children may be brought up without hearing the word. To damn a person or wish him in Hell may be considered merely an outburst in poor taste.[1] When Lowes Dickinson wrote that he could not be happy in Heaven if he thought there were inmates in Hell he expressed a not uncommon feeling. At any rate the conception of torturing the dead is less gratifying to us than to our ancestors.

[1] In poorer taste for a woman, let us note, than for a man. Swearing gives a sense or suggestion of power that is deemed unseemly in a woman. When the wife of Moses à Vauts "let fly 2 or 3 bloudy, horrid Oaths" in his face, he tells us: "I bestowed so many Flaps with my bare hand alone on her Mouth, the Part offending; . . . Neither did I offer this, but on the same Terms I will gladly accept the like, from any Christian other than my Wife, whatever." (*The Husband's Authority Unvail'd;* "Wherein It is moderately discussed whether it be fit or lawful for a *good Man,* to beat his *bad Wife,*" p. 84. London 1650.)

Historically, swearing is an appeal to the gods, a vicarious resort to power often taboo to women.

# THE GODS

THE dead are dependent upon the living and bound to their service. Equally if not more dependent and subject are the gods. Some of them are credited to be sure with a will of their own, and that will must be humoured. On the other hand far more is likely to be expected of the gods than of the dead.

These expectations begin to be raised with the deified dead. Ancestor gods, apotheosised chiefs or kings, are required to bring down blessings of all kinds upon their people—to bring them rain, to still high winds, to cause abundant harvests, to cause increase in the flocks or herds, to give victory over the enemy—to do for the people even more, far more, than was asked of them in life as divinely endowed rulers.

The sacred, representative sovereign is to be viewed in the present connection as a subject divinity. He is endowed with mystical powers in order to employ them in behalf of his so-called "subjects." Such a misnomer together with the emotional disguise accompanying it, let us note incidentally, is a not uncommon method of *de facto* rulers to maintain control. This sentimental device is sometimes apparent for example in referring to a mate as a mistress or a "better half," in imputing influence to women over men in general, particularly to women in public affairs, the backstairs influence.

Loyalty to a chief is often an analogous paraphrase for making use of him, for making him do the work. Recently, for example, appeals have been made for loyalty to the American Executive in a situation where his *subjects* have been loath to take the trouble[1] to decide each for himself. That diplomacy, the handling of international affairs, should have been left so completely in the hands of the people's *representatives* means, not an usurpation of power by the representatives, but a desire on the part of the sovereign people to es-

[1] Or to be courageous enough. Cp. Lippmann, *The Stakes of Diplomacy*, pp. 34-7.

cape thinking or acting upon matters they hold of little or no interest.

The better to assure themselves of this immunity, the sovereign people hold their representatives strictly to their functions and in many ways restrict their liberties. The restrictions furthermore gratify the people's will to power. Like other subject types, representative "rulers" must dress, diet, talk, behave, move about, and mate in general in prescribed ways. They must marry or not marry [1] for the good of the State or in accordance with public opinion. They must hold themselves aloof, living more or less segregated, not making themselves "common" or "cheap." In short they must live with great prudence and circumspection. They must never forget their position or the dignity due their office, *i. e.*, no matter what the personal inconvenience they must come up to their people's expectations.

[1] To give an American illustration, let us suppose a President of the United States who had become a widower while in office were to contemplate remarriage. Would he not be severely criticised? It would be said, would it not, that by remarrying within a short period he was setting a bad example in cherishing the memory of the dead and that at any rate in the midst of momentous public affairs he ought not turn his attention to private matters.

The people want someone to look up to and to
look to, they want someone to serve their interests, to bring them good weather, good crops, and
good business, good health and good morals.
And they want someone to control others for .
them, enemies abroad and at home.   Such a vicarious control is one of the most important functions of representative rulership.   It is indeed
so important that the need of it has only to
seem urgent enough to reinstate in power a
decadent monarchy or an administration out of
favour.

Once the principle of vicarious control departs
from kingship, kingship is threatened.   To keep
his subjects content a king must give them a sense
of power through his power.   Let the divine right
of kings become merely self-assertive and the
people will clamour for a more representative form
of government.   They will strive to assert their
own will through a constitution.   If they feel their
divine king is no longer a go-between for them
with the gods, that he brings them poverty instead of wealth, bad weather instead of good,
defeat instead of victory, they may even try to

get rid of him altogether—to kill him[1] or depose him.

As for representative rulers themselves, would they be free from subjection to the people's will, there is but one escape for them, and not for all of them—abdication or refusal to take office. A Massai to be made a chief has to be first captured. Otherwise, resentful of being put into the class of old men, the proper classification for chiefs, he would run away.[2] So onerous were the taboos upon the rulers of Angoy, Bastian reports, that at the time of his visit to that African kingdom the kingship had gone begging for ten years.[3] Since the day after the King of Ngoio takes the cap (the crown) he is killed, the throne of Ngoio is permanently vacant.[4]

Dead, even refusal to take or hold office is not open to the personages people would worship. The dead have to lend themselves to their cult

---

[1] But regicide is not merely a punishment for thwarting the popular will. Divine kings, like other subject classes, may be killed as a direct expression of the collective will. See Frazer, *Kingship*, pp. 291 ff.

[2] Hollis, A. C., *The Massai*, p. 300. Oxford, 1905.

[3] *Die Deutsche Expedition an der Loango-Küste*, p. 368. Jena, 1874.        [4] Dennett, p. xxxii.

whether they would or not. Self-determinism in this particular is not open to any of the gods. All are subject to the will of their worshippers. In other particulars, however, certain gods are less amenable than others. Out and out nature gods are less docile than ancestor gods. Nature gods have a little more will of their own; their conduct is more uncertain, less responsible. But they can be placated, coaxed, wheedled, and by a kind of nagging, by persistent prayer and present making, forced into the routine expected of them. They or their proxies can even be killed, as in ancient Mexico or in Phœnicia or in Judea, to serve as intercessors with the high gods or as vicarious sufferers or as regulators of the seasons or of reproduction.

Seasonal or weather gods seem to be peculiarly subject to drastic treatment. "It is said that in the reign of Kia-King, fifth emperor of the Manchu dynasty, a long drought desolated several provinces of Northern China. Processions were of no avail; the rain-dragon hardened his heart and would not let a drop fall. At last the emperor lost patience and condemned the recalcitrant

deity to perpetual exile on the banks of the river
Illi. The decree was in process of execution: the
divine criminal, with a touching resignation, was
already traversing the deserts of Tartary to work
out his sentence on the borders of Turkestan, when
the judges of the high court of Peking, moved with
compassion, flung themselves at the foot of the
emperor and implored his pardon for the poor
devil. The emperor consented to revoke his doom,
and a messenger set off at full gallop to bear the
tidings of mercy to the executors of the imperial
justice. The dragon was reinstated in his office
on condition of performing his duties a little better
in future. In April, 1888, the mandarins of Can-
ton prayed to the god Lung-wong to stop the incessant downpour of rain; and when he turned a
deaf ear to their petitions they put him in a lock-
up for five days. This had a salutary effect.
The rain ceased and the god was restored to liberty.
Some years before, in time of drought, the same
deity had been chained and exposed to the sun for
days in the courtyard of his temple in order that
he might feel for himself the urgent need of rain.
So when the Siamese are in want of rain, they set

out their idols in the blazing sun; but if they need
dry weather, they unroof the temples and let the
rain pour down on the idols.   They think that
the inconvenience to which the gods are thus sub-
jected by the inclemency of the weather will induce
them to grant the wishes of their worshippers."[1]

Nor, as Frazer points out, is this treatment of
rain-making spirits peculiar to the Orient.  The
Catholic Saint may suffer it.   In Sicily, in 1893,
there was a great drought.   By the end of April,
propitiatory measures having failed, the people
turned on their rain-sending saints.   "At Palermo
they dumped St. Joseph in a garden to see the
state of things for himself, and they swore to leave
him there in the sun till rain fell.  Other saints were
turned, like naughty children, with their faces to
the wall.   Others again, stripped of their beautiful
robes, were exiled far from their parishes, threatened, grossly insulted, ducked in horse-ponds.   At
Caltanisetta the golden wings of St. Michael the
Archangel were torn from his shoulders and re-
placed with wings of pasteboard: his purple mantle
was taken away and a clout wrapt about him

[1] Frazer, *Kingship*, pp. 98–99.

instead. At Licata the patron saint, St. Angelo, fared even worse, for he was left without any garments at all: he was reviled, he was put in irons, he was threatened with drowning or hanging. 'Rain or the rope!' roared the angry people at him, as they shook their fists in his face. "[1]

If a spirit remain too refractory, he is likely to get a bad name that will stick, he is called an evil spirit, a demon, a devil. Was not our own arch fiend but a rebellious spirit, rebellious against the deity who heeded and cared for mankind? And yet, although Satan and his followers were cast down from heaven and relations with him stigmatised, he was still called upon to do men service—to be sure at a high price. Outside of the peoples inheriting Asiatic myths of dualism, the powers of evil are openly propitiated and through such propitiation kept more or less in hand. The existence of irretrievably bad, utterly unruly gods may be regarded as a confession of weakness worshippers are loath to make. Most gods, like most people, have some good in them if you only know how to get at it.

[1] Frazer, *Kingship*, p. 101.

Getting at it is difficult enough, to be sure, to require expert talent. As a rule the gods must have their priests. Most peoples have delegated the care and management of their gods to a priesthood. Only through their priesthood may the people control their gods. Such an attempt as was the Protestant Reformation to get at grips with deity is rare. And even the Protestants did not dispense altogether with a sacerdotal go-between. They merely lessened the degree of vicariousness in their control. The management is still left to their priesthood by the Protestant sects on many occasions—at christenings, marriages, funerals, and at a weekly "service."

In expert priestly hands it is not remarkable that supernaturalism flourished in spite of the extremely vicarious character of its gratifications. It is to the interest of the sacerdotal group to make both the gods and their worshippers dependent upon them. By enhancing and extending the powers of the gods they enhance and extend their own priestly powers, getting more gratification thereby from their control over worshippers. And a supernaturally  powerful priesthood and powerful pantheon gratify vicariously the worshippers. The more power your gods have, the more they can do for you and enable you to do. Hence the more masterful your gods, the more masterful are you—a signal illustration, all this, of the vicarious principle.

The gods are constrained to the service of priests and worshippers in much the same way non-supernatural creatures are constrained. They too have wants. They need victuals and clothes and shelter, slaves and servants. Often they are assumed to need not only divine wives, but human, and women are dedicated to them.

To the wives, slaves, and servants of the gods attach the same restrictions as to the wives, slaves, and servants of their worshippers—only in greater degree. Labour, preclusion from "outside interests," continence or, out of compliment to the phallic nature of a deity, incontinence, a special dress, a special tonsure, a special diet, a special bearing or behaviour, *i. e.*, devout or pious or reverential manners—manners which satisfy the divine desires for obedience and servility. Religious asceticism, fasting, mutilation, self-sacri-

10

fice, self-abasement, a lowly and humble spirit, reverence, awe, are all recognitions of the will to power of ambitious and overbearing gods.

Despite these indulgences, the gods, *ex hypothesi* the most arbitrary and self-assertive of gods, are kept in leash. They are allowed no interests apart from those of their worshippers. They have to live even more intensively at second hand than women or slaves. What tastes they have they may never change. Their characteristics or attributes are fixed. Their provinces are fixed and their status. As Pliny once pointed out, the gods may not even commit suicide.

Men give to the gods the powers they covet for themselves, and the temper and bearing they would be possessed of. They give the gods the same nature and the same interests, for only through such similarities can they get at their gods. The god who is remote from men's interests is unapproachable. He is perforce let alone, becoming a negligible high god.

In other words, a god must take an interest, otherwise he can't be appealed to. And so his kinship, his tribal fatherhood, is insisted upon, and he is believed to be vitally concerned over the least of his creatures. Nor can a god change or widen his interests—safely. Were he to become the father of all mankind, for example, it would be difficult for one section of mankind to appeal to him against another section. His interest in so many men would keep him from being the abettor of a few. It would be hard to make him take sides.

In the present European war God has had to show himself very plainly as a group figure, a national personage. Christian monotheism has been overtly denied by Christian nationals.[1] But neither in Christendom nor elsewhere has monotheism ever really existed as a religion, a system of action, it has existed only as a philosophy, a system of thought. Practically, polytheism has ever

---

[1] *I. e.*, by Christian belligerents. By those under less stress, by non-belligerents, an international god is still posited. Referring to what the German government has called its "sacred" duty Miss Repplier remarks: "The German is certainly at home in Zion. If his god be a trifle exacting in the matter of human sacrifice, he is otherwise the most pliant and accommodating of deities. It is one of our many disadvantages that we have no American god, only the Divinity, whose awful name is, by common consent, omitted [as a high god] from diplomatic correspondence." (*Counter-Currents*, p. 239.)

been necessary, necessary not only in inter-group relations but within the same group. Within the group polytheism has seemed as necessary as polygamy. In supernaturalism as in marriage there had to be a division of labour, and of appeal. There may be a nominal kind of monotheism, as there is a nominal monogamy, but flirtations with demigods, with saints, even with fairies, are sure to occur. One must not ask too much of divine nature. To be sure when science comes to the relief of religion, taking over many of its functions, monotheism appears more possible—just as the wage-earning system made the existence of mono-gamy more possible. A still freer economic sys-tem may make monogamy quite possible, but, in so far as it is a legal system, undesired. Develop-ments of science may also make religion quite monotheistic—and superfluous.

But another outcome for religion is also possible. The increasing disuse of the gods in our culture is due far less to rationalism than to their own failure to make good. Theology has failed to develop, to keep pace with modern culture. In early culture stability was required of the gods, as we have noted; they had to give their worshippers an assurance of unchangeableness, some protection against the dynamics of nature or society. They had to supply sanctions for conservatism, and be examples of it. Early man was very fearful of change. For protection against it he looked largely to his gods. But modern man is less timorous. He welcomes change or at least simulates a welcome. At any rate when he succeeds in viewing change as progress he is not panic-struck about it.

Of this change of cultural attitude at least two warnings were served to theologians. Failure of belief in the doctrine of predestination was one notice, conversion to the doctrine of evolution was another. In the doctrine of predestination the divine autocracy went too far for the modern spirit of mastery. People wanted to have a hand in their fate and this desire was even greater than the desire to be assured of a divinely appointed order, a divine mitigation of change. In other words people were becoming willing to put up with the uncertainties of an unforeordained world if only they could take part in determining those uncer-

tainties. A preordaining almighty god no longer
served them, he was alike too inaccessible and too
powerful, so they repudiated him. This they did
the more easily because of the substitute offered
them, the doctrine of evolution. Evolutionary
theory took them in somewhat as partners, gave
them the opportunity to co-operate in making
changes the old theological determinism had denied
them. And yet the doctrine of evolution was
sufficiently deterministic not to alarm its converts.
It provided for change, but only for orderly, de-
sirable change, for a teleological progress.[1]

For a long time the theologians fought against
the usurpation of divine government the doctrine
of evolution meant to them. At last they had wit
enough to drop vain antagonism and look for
reconciliation, but by the time they came to call
evolution God's instrument it was too late to
recover the lost worshippers. They had got on
too satisfactorily with the godless belief that so
tickled their own sense of mastery.

Of recent years in scientific circles the dogma

[1] Parsons, E. C., "Circumventing Darwinism," *Jour. Philosophy, Psychology and Scientific Methods*, Oct. 28, 1915.

of evolution has been challenged. As applied to human mind at least it has been somewhat discredited. Many anthropologists hold that mind has not evolved—at least since its achievements have been put on record. This conclusion is necessarily a blow to the will to power of educator and of social reformer. Their faith will be at a low ebb once this non-evolutionary tenet is popularised. In self-protection they will seek new sources of inspiration and re-enforcement. Then will be the psychological moment for the introduction of a new god, a god of progress, a god who will accept change and sanction it, a god who will make life pleasanter for radicals and reformers, who will intensify their faith and confirm their devotion.

Already the metaphysic of ethnology is ripe for this divine appearance. Mind evolves not, but culture does evolve, certain ethnologists are declaring. Culture is an entity, I heard one of them not long since asserting, culture is a self-determining entity, "call it God if you like." Surely, given this opportune state of mind, once more the gods may become the servants of man, doing his will on the ground that it is their own.

# SELF

THE common phrases, *self-control, self-mastery, self-indulgence, self-discipline*, would of themselves suggest, quite irrespective of our systematic moral philosophy, that oneself is accounted a fit subject for the exercise of one's will. The displays of will over self, self-will, to change the point of view generally held in using that term, are curiously like the displays of will in controlling others. We do things to ourselves, to body and mind, we pamper and doctor ourselves, we ornament and improve ourselves. We work for ourselves—for our old age, as we say—or we take a vow of poverty or we enslave ourselves. We play games[1] with ourselves or play against our record.

---

[1] Veblen has analysed the satisfaction we get from games as indulgence of our emulative predatory impulses in conspicuously non-productive activity, a token, like all ostentatious waste, of wealth or economic power. But games should be analysed also as an indulgence of the will to power favoured by immunity from consequences. A game is self-sufficient, self-limiting. From this point of view may be interpreted many rules of the game and

We make heroes of ourselves, in dream or awake. Sometimes we segregate ourselves, turning anchorite or, in trance, casting the body aside altogether. Likewise, ascetically disposed, we neglect or starve or beat or mutilate ourselves. We take self-regarding vows or pledges, making promises to ourselves. We show ourselves off—perversely, as we say, in acts of exhibitionism or in the still more puerile psychical ways of showing off characteristic of children and women. There is sexual self-excitation. Enterprise in self-impregnation is not unknown. There is self-killing. Losing control of ourselves in some way we feel thwarted or

---

much of the spirit of fair play. To play fairly, no appeal may be made to social classification—that indulgence, in justice to the game, should be superfluous. Consequently, if you are not willing to forego even temporarily the advantages of such classification you will play only with your peers. You won't play with a girl or with a servant or with a subject. When in the middle of a game of tennis Francis I. called out to the gentleman playing against him and accusing him of a foul, "Darest thou contradict a king?" and forthwith stabbed the gentleman, Francis, we would all agree, proved himself a poor sport. To play the game you must not only be a good loser, you must also be a magnanimous winner. You must not boast or rub it in. You play, not to conquer, if you are a true sport,—an Englishman, shall we say, not an American,—you play not even to win, you play merely for the pleasure of the contest. The paramount and peculiar charm of games is the opportunity they afford for an impersonal, inconsequential exercise of will.

diminished by the loss of self-control—whether through temper or through alcohol or narcotics or through hypnotism.

This dualistic fancifulness I would not exaggerate, it is far too complex a state of mind to lend itself, except by verbal play, to any analysis of self-will we may undertake. Two subjects it has opened, however, suicide and asceticism, which do invite us even for the moment to further consideration.

Several types of suicide may be regarded as endeavour to recover a sense of power that has been lost. Suicide from temper or passion is a reaction from being thwarted coupled with the feeling that one can have one's way again at least by suicide.[1]

---

[1] Self-mutilation may be similarly motivated. Violently angry a Kallan of Madura may tear in two the strips of flesh which constitute the dilated lobe of his ear. (Thurston, p. 372.) We hear of a Hindu *sadhu* who in a rage publicly castrated himself to get rid of a nagging wife and escape the jeers of his fellow ascetics. (Oman, J. C., *The Mystics, Ascetics, and Saints of India* p. 48. London, 1903.) "If thy right eye offend thee, pluck it out. . . . If thy right hand offend thee, cut it off."

These are instances or counsels of self-mutilation to get the better of oneself or of another. The passionate, ear-splitting Kallan expects to compel his adversary to imitate his act. The European duel is an analogous attempt to force the hand of an adversary. This aspect of the will to power is apparent too in forcing an enemy to go to war or, as in Burma, to expose your

This seems to be the psychology of the enraged
Chukchee who has himself killed by his family or
of the Hindu creditor who threatens to starve
himself to death unless he is paid or of the Tshi
who kills himself "on the head of another"[1] or of
the Chinaman who kills himself at his enemy's door.
The Chinaman believes that after death he can re-
venge himself far better than in life.   Promised by
the God Mahādeva that in return for her austerities
she shall be reborn a warrior the better to destroy
her enemy Bhishma, the princess Amvā of Benares
has a great funeral pyre raised up on the river bank
and, setting fire to it, plunges into the blaze "with
a heart burning with wrath, uttering the words,
'I do so for Bhishma's destruction.'"[2]   A type of

person indecently in order to make your enemy do likewise.
(Brown, R. G., "Burman Modesty," in *Man*, Sept., 1915.)
It would be an interesting experiment in Burma to decline the
challenge of exposure.  Of like interest would be the experiment
of a nation declining to engage in war.  In Germany, if being
*satisfactionfähig*, you decline a challenge your challenger is disgraced—under such circumstances a German officer must leave
the army.  If you were too wilful to expose your person or to
go to war, too modest or too proud, what would be the effect on
your adversary?

[1] Ellis, A. B., *The Tshi-Speaking Peoples of the Gold Coast of
West Africa*, p. 302.  London, 1887.  He whom the intending
suicide has termed the cause of his act is killed by the same
form of death.                                    [2] Oman, pp. 21-2.

suicide related perhaps to the Oriental type, although less definite or standardized, is killing yourself to make another person *feel bad*.

To escape from the design of another may be also an object in suicide. Thus, rather than take part in a gladiatorial show Symmachus the prefect was holding, his Saxon prisoners strangled themselves in prison. Similarly in the reign of Richard First the Jews of York killed themselves rather than be killed by the Christians of York—an outcome since repeated in other instances of Jew-baiting. In the present European war we have heard of cases of killing oneself rather than obeying the order to kill others.

Even the less specifically motivated suicide, the suicide from the feeling that shabbily or treacherously as life has dealt one, one can at least leave it, even this suicide of despair is a wilful act. It lies in one's power after all not to be wholly overcome by life. "Against all the injuries of life," wrote Seneca, "I have the refuge of death." In short it may fairly be said that suicide is in many cases a last desperate act of self-assertion.

The sense of power that comes of ascetic practices I must also content myself with merely indicating; it is a complex the psychologist may some day notice. Some day he may explain the gratification that comes of spending a lifetime on top of a pillar or on a bed of spikes or in mire or water. He may explain the satisfaction from standing for ever on one's toes or with arm or leg uplifted until it withers or from loading down one's body with ball and chain or from journeying hundreds of miles by prostration, inchworm fashion. He may tell us what was the return to Simeon Stylites, to Anthony, to Bhaskarananda Saraswati; what the sense of achievement or control to the Russian Skopzi, to the Moslem faquir, to the Hindu *sadhu;* and why the Puritan felt he was acquiring merit in taking life hard.

In India and elsewhere there is evidence that the power realised is not confined to power over oneself; nature and the gods are compelled to compliance by ascetic practices. It was his abstinence from meat, Apollonius declared, that gave him his gift of prophecy.[1] To force deity to grant his prayer the Tsimshian Indian of British Columbia

[1] Lecky, I., 391 n. 4.

fasts[1] for four or for seven days and keeps apart from his wife.[2] In struggles between Hindu *sadhus* and the gods, to the greater ascetic belongs the victory. So great were the self-tortures of King Visvamitra that he was able to create new stars and to threaten the gods with new gods. Finally, having maintained absolute silence and suspended breathing for hundreds of years, smoke began to issue from his head, "to the great consternation of the three worlds." The gods and the *rishis* then addressed Brahma, the high god: "The great *muni* Visvamitra has been allured and provoked in various ways, but still advances in his sanctity. If his wish is not conceded, he will destroy the three worlds by the force of his austerity." To preclude this catastrophe Brahma is constrained to grant the wish of the mighty ascetic

---

[1] Is it fanciful to see in the hunger strike of English suffragettes something of this spirit, government taking the place of deity? When it is alleged by Roosevelt and others that individual self-control brings about national control, "a manifestation of the highest civilisation," Civilisation appears to be the entity that is constrained by the ascetic spirit.

[2] Boas, F., in *Rep. Brit. Assn. Adv. Sc.*, 1889, pp. 846-7.

Was it to force the hand of the deity our Anglo-Saxon forebears decreed days of fasting such as was decreed, for example, by the New York Assembly on September 26, 1691, "on account of the burdensome war and the blast on corn"?

and promote him to the rank of Brahmanhood.[1]
Brahmans themselves add to their power by asceticism. Thanks to their vow of chastity eighty
thousand Brahman sages once obtained immor-
tality and the power to accomplish their wishes by
conceiving them, "for instance the desire to procure rain, to bestow children, second sight, to
move quick as thought, and other desires of this
description."[2]

This Brahmanic concept is close, I surmise, to
the far more general notions underlying religious vows, specifically the vow to maltreat oneself. The vow is a means to achievement. A
Hindu will vow to "swing"[3] if he marry a certain girl within a certain time. An expectant
mother will take a like vow if her child be a boy.
To get what they want Fuhchan women will

[1] Oman, pp. 29–30.
[2] *Āpastamba*, II., 9, 23, vv. 5–7. *Sacred Books of the East;*
Parsons, *Religious Chastity*, p. 314.
[3] By hooks through the flesh of his back, (Thurston, p. 493).
*Ex-voto* mutilation is not always mutilation of self. In Southern India a woman who has lost a child may vow to name an
expected child after the god or goddess at Tirupati. The infant
is accordingly taken to the temple, its hair is removed and the
lobe of its ear pierced. Under like circumstances a Nayar child
has his nose slit. (*Ib.*, p. 368.)

vow to eat nothing but rice for a month or a
year.[1]

Whether or not because asceticism gives power
over deity and so interferes with the prerogatives
of priesthoods who secure power by unascetic
measures, asceticism is likely to be discouraged by
the churches. The Brahmans disapprove of such
extreme measures as hook-swinging. The early
Christian hierarchy condemned self-castration.
In later periods self-flagellants were persecuted.
Indeed except when asceticism, and let me add
suicide, have been planned or dictated by the
group itself, the group is disposed to be down on
these expressions of individual will. They interfere with the collective will. The prejudice
against an unbroken individual rule of chastity
may be thus in part explained. (Likewise the
uncritical vehemence against masturbation or
against "solitary" drinking.) As for self-murder,
"a man's life does not belong to himself," we say,
it belongs to the king, say the Dahomans,[2] and

---

[1] Doolittle, II., 186.

[2] Ellis, A. B., *The Ewe-Speaking Peoples of the Slave Coast of West Africa*, p. 224. London, 1890.

both they and we classify suicide as crime, treating the would-be suicide as a criminal. He has encroached upon the king's right or the group's[1] right to kill.[2]

In the Goajira Peninsula of Colombia any physical self-injury, accidental or otherwise, is also a crime. The maternal relatives of the man who has hurt himself demand blood-money. Being of their blood he is not allowed to spill it without paying. His father's people demand "tear-money." Friends present ask to be compensated for their sorrow at seeing their friend in pain. The instrument that caused the accident may be appropriated by any one. The pay is in ratio to the injury. "A slightly cut finger is settled with a little Indian corn, a kid, or such

[1] Formerly the encroachment was against God, since life, as Thomas Aquinas put it, is "subject to His power who 'killeth and maketh alive.'"

[2] Where no encroachment is suspected, no crime is imputed. Starvation is commonly tolerated by the community, for example, when it is an involuntary experience. So is suicide as, for example, in the classical custom of condemning political prisoners to kill themselves or in the Japanese custom of making *harakiri* obligatory upon Samurai criminals or in the modern German fashion of expecting an officer unable to pay a gambling debt to fall from his horse or "accidentally" to shoot himself.

11

trifle. A bad cut requires at least a goat or a sheep with other sundries."[1]

. That one's body does not belong to oneself is a view taken quite commonly about the subject classes. "The body is that which has been transmitted to us by our parents; dare any one allow himself to be irreverent in the employment of their legacy?" To this Chinese query the answer is: "A man's parents give birth to his person all complete, and to return it to them all complete may be called filial duty. When no member has been mutilated and no disgrace done to any part of the person, it may be called complete, and hence a superior man does not dare to take the slightest step in forgetfulness of his filial duty. . . . A son should not forget his parents in a single lifting up of his feet, and therefore he will walk in the highway and not take a by-path, he will use a boat and not attempt to wade through a stream;—not daring, with the body left him by his parents, to go in the way of peril."[2]   Analo-

[1] Simons, F. A. A., in *Proc. Roy. Geog. Soc.*, N. S. VII. (1885), 790.
[2] *Lî Kî, Sacred Books of the East*, XXVIII., 226–9.

gously the Anglo-Saxon churl who left the place assigned to him was held to have stolen his own body. He could be summarily hanged when caught.[1] Perhaps modern law is still affected by Paul's dogma that "a wife hath not power over her body, but her husband."

In conclusion let me suggest that the student of asceticism would do well to consider certain types of self-privation which figure in codes of good manners or in etiquette. I mean such rules as the Tavetan man's rule against eating birds, birds being food fit only for women and children,[2] or as the Kwakiutl rule against drinking water at meals, that satisfaction being left to the young and to those of humble condition,[3] or as the rule in genteel Yankee circles to leave something on your plate and not to ask for a "second help" if you wish to be considered polite and well brought up.[4] Rather than ask for more the Eastern American will leave the table hungry, rather than drink at

[1] Pike, I., 90.
[2] Hollis, in *J. A. S.*, I. (1901–2), 104 n. 1.
[3] Boas, F., in *Mem. Amer. Mus. Nat. Hist.*, V., 427, 428.
[4] Such evidences of gentility are not completely explained as a corollary of Veblen's theory of conspicuous consumption.

the wrong time the North-Western American will choke to death. Conformity to the rules of *noblesse oblige* gives, I surmise, if only in slight degree, that sense of superiority which is a sense of power.

# THE SATISFACTION FROM SCIENCE

HAS it surprised the reader that in the view of social rule I have been trying to present I have found more to say about the ruled than the ruler, that to elders and chiefs, to wardens and judges, to priests and deities, I have not paid much direct attention, and that when I have, it was generally to suggest that these so-called ruling classes are, in fact, at times, subject classes? Believing that this aspect of social rulers, *i. e.*, their own subjugation, has been overlooked, I have been disposed to emphasise it, perhaps, I confess, to exaggerate it. Similarly, believing that political rule has received attention out of proportion to other forms of social rule I have been disposed to neglect its discussion. So prominent indeed is the conception of political freedom in our modern culture, so overbearing we may say, that other forms of social freedom get little or no purposive consideration or conscious interest. We go so far as to say and even think we are a *free people* if we live in a political democracy or even in a nominal political democracy. For oppressions of age-class by age-class, of sex by sex, of caste by caste, of minorities of all kinds by majorities, we have little or no concern. And yet how influential in the daily life of each of us are these covert and overlooked tyrannies!

It is to these tyrannies I have wished to direct attention, and to that end our current ideas of the ruling classes had to be somewhat revised. We had to see not only how much they expressed the principle of vicarious rule, but that even so exercise of social power is not confined to their hands. Conspicuous concentrations of power the professional ruling classes may grasp for and command, but social power is vastly diffused.

The principle or method of vicariousness we have but glanced at in this study, yet it is, I feel assured, one of the most important factors in social control. More than any other principle it keeps the ruling classes in power. Bringing a certain amount of satisfaction to the individual it leads him to relinquish personal power. In this way the principle of vicarious rule may be truly important too in the development of culture. Unrestrained individual striving for power in an immature culture is pregnant with dangers. Its actual havoc may be seen in the practice of black magic. Fearful as are the ravages of religion, the ravages of magic appear to be even greater. Now although priesthoods may work magic, and the layman may perform religious rites, on the whole, magic is more of an individualistic and direct search for influence or power and religion more of a collectivistic and vicarious search. Through its vicarious character religion is a constraint in a simple, uncritical society upon personal, anti-social ambitions, ambitions such as we find sometimes articulate in the boastings of little children or as we see pictured in the traits or deeds attributed to heroes of folktale or legend. A community is far better off possessed of a single rain-making god or chief than, like the Akikuyu, of a whole clan with the power of foreseeing rain and stopping it.[1] Women who have only a single deity to pro-

[1] Routledge, p. 22.

pitiate in the matter of childbearing must live in a state of less anxiety than women who feel that any man who takes a grudge against them may wish them a child when they do not want one or may keep from them the child they desire.

, Next in importance to the method or factor of vicariousness is the factor of multiple gratification. I call the gratification multiple because it may indulge the will to power in more than one way or indulge more than one class of persons. Breeding dogs or dwarfs or slaves, or buying slave girls as concubines, or deifying animals or women or children, or sacrificing subject creatures to the dead or to the gods, torturing them for magical ends, [1] all these customs are illustrations of the first-mentioned form of indulgence. Among other even more complex instances one might cite castrating slaves to provide guards for the harem, or employing dogs or birds to hunt or fish, or

---

[1] For example, a Blackfellow whose wife has run away from him with another man will catch a rabbit-bandicoot with young in her pouch. He dislocates both her hip joints and leaves her helpless on the ground. As the animal slowly dies the runaway wife is supposed to waste away. (Spencer, B., and Gillen, F. J., *The Northern Tribes of Central Australia*, p. 466. London and New York, 1904.)

condemning criminals to combats with wild beasts or, also in antique fashion, to suicide, or, as in Dahomey, sending delinquent women to war, or mortifying the flesh to compel the gods to service. Of this latter type of multiple gratification, of doing something to oneself to compel results in others, out of abounding cases I may cite the Haida or the Tshi who paints herself white or who fasts when her husband goes to war, or the Jew who fasts that God may send his daughter a husband, or the Fuhchan woman who goes without her breakfast for a stated time that her husband may become rich or learned.

The indulgence gratifying to more than one class of persons we noted as characteristic of the rule of seniority—there being almost always a junior to coerce or lord it over—and we noted an analogous gratification in the advantage accruing to matrons from the sex subjection of girls. Marital control may gratify priests and their gods. Joining the hands of the bridal pair the Armenian priest says to the groom: "According to the divine order which God gave to our ancestors, I, a priest, give thee now this wife in subjection. Wilt thou be her master?" The groom replies: "With the help of God, I will." Turning to the bride, the priest asks: "Wilt thou be obedient to him?" She answers: "I am obedient according to the order of God."[1] Milton's Eve is even more concise: "God is thy law, thou mine."

Apart from the particular subjection promised, marriage vows are merely as vows[2] a form of multiple gratification. So are sacrifices. Sacrifices to the gods or to the dead gratify those who make the sacrifice as well as those who receive it. Classification by caste and classification by time of arrival abound in multiple gratifications. Patronising or snubbing is never confined to one caste and there is always a last comer to put in his place.

Through such combination outlets the will to power proves itself highly effluent. It flows on

---

[1] Garnett, Lucy M. A., *The Women of Turkey; the Christian Women*, p. 238. London, 1890.

[2] The more the vow approaches a contract, an exchange of values, the less is it a form of subjection; but the indefinite pledge, the mere promise, "never to do it again" or to be good or loving or loyal is an overt and in itself gratifying submission to the will of another, to the will of Elder or spouse or chief or god. That is one reason why a broken promise, perhaps even a broken treaty, is so exasperating.

seemingly indifferent to the direction it takes. The indifference appears characteristic of the group as well as of the individual, *i. e.*, the collective will takes one institutional form and then another. In one society the young are set to work, in another, they are *improved*. Sometimes the improvement consists of inculcating doctrine, sometimes of using charms against black magic. In one society women are *supported*, in another they are beaten or mutilated. This culture is slaveholding, that culture favours military conscription or prostitution or convict labour. Here we have funeral sacrifice or gladiatorial combat, there prize-fighting or cock-fighting or Jew-baiting. Sometimes the dead are the more hard worked, sometimes the gods. Belief in punishment after death may lessen the desire to punish the living.[1] The feeling that "you will be sorry some day" may take the place of wanting to make you sorry today.

Not only does one kind of oppression substitute

[1] May we not suppose that the Hindu who believes that his disobedient wife will be a jackal or even a wretched widow in her next incarnation will be less drastic, other things being equal, than a husband lacking this comforting assurance?

for another kind as, for example, chivalry[1] for marital proprietorship, slavery for polygyny, a bureaucracy for an aristocracy, democratic standardisation for caste restrictions; an achieved freedom may lead directly to fresh tyranny. Emancipated from their elders, the junior age-class may start in to tyrannise over the senior age-classes. Establish woman's right to a job and new forms of sex subjection may ensue.[2] Give the wage-earner an economic stake and you may enslave "backward" peoples. Who can doubt that if modern psychical research established means of communicating with the dead, their freedom, whatever it is, would be gravely jeopardised. As it is they are expected to attend the kind of social gathering and talk the trivialities they probably learned how to escape in life. A spirit at a *séance* is in worse plight than a woman or, at any rate, a man at an afternoon reception.

Given this facility in transformation or trans-

[1] *See* Parsons, *Fear and Conventionality*, pp. 76–7, for a brief consideration of the sense of power from chivalry.

[2] Plato suggested such an outcome for feminist reform. Having planned that women should share in military interests and in men's general way of life he recommends that woman's nature be *made* as nearly as possible like the nature of man. (*Timæus*, 18.)

mutation of the will to power,[1] is there any outlook at all for social freedom, any escape ahead from social tyranny? I think there is. But the escape is not what we usually plan in our utter devotion to rationalising ethics. The escape will not be through an increase of social justice in itself or even through a greater direct desire for social freedom. No student of the rationalising of social desire can have much belief in the independent development of ethics. In the long run a people does what it wants to do and what it wants to do it thinks right.[2] The ethical or cultural

---

[1] Failure to appreciate this facility makes moralists marvel at the "capricious and inconsistent" displays of "humanity," that may be seen in any society, makes Lecky, for example, wonder why nets were spread out under Roman rope-dancers during a period "when the blood of captives was poured out like water in the Colosseum." (*European Morals*, I., 308.) Killing was not the particular gratification a Roman derived from tight-rope exhibitions.

[2] One of the most striking illustrations of this point of view is the attitude of the Christian Church to slavery. It is said that not one of the Fathers even hints that slavery is improper. The martyrs possessed slaves; bishops and popes, monasteries and churches possessed them. Slaves were bought and sold "in the name of God." The Church urged devotees to enslave their bodies, as church documents put it, in order to procure the liberty of their souls. A seventh century Council decreed that the bastards of priests should become the slaves of their fathers' churches. The slaves of monasteries were everywhere the last to be manumitted. Similarly, the American churches were said

changes necessary to greater freedom will come
about mainly through a diversion of the will to
power from human beings to nature, a diversion
that is obviously not novel, that has been going on
always, but that began to receive a very great im-
petus with the rise of modern science

Modern science offers three main outlets to our
energy—power over the inanimate, over nature,
power over the animate, over other creatures, and
in particular power over our own mental processes.
Ratiocination gives in itself a sense of power or
achievement. The charm of generalising is the
feeling of capacity or of control it imparts. To
certain types of mind it is far more satisfying to
classify or marshal facts than to "place" human
beings, and the sense of power that comes from
comprehension of reality rivals or surpasses that
felt by ruling other persons. Many a modern
scientist would have been in an earlier culture, I

to be the bulwarks of American slavery. Churchmen asserted
that slavery was founded on the judgment of God on a damned
race, the descendants of Ham, and that only through slavery
could the African share in the blessings of Christianity and civilisation. (Westermarck, I., 694 ff.).—English cock-fighting was
once justified on the ground that cocks had thus to suffer for
St. Peter's crime. (*Ib.*, II., 509.)

suspect, a ruler of men. But even in the earlier cultures the acquirement of knowledge must be in itself a source of gratification. Quite apart from the satisfaction of practising it, magic imparts, I surmise, a sense of power. Any knowledge, magical or scientific, is not only power, practical power, it gratifies intellectually the will to power. It is not surprising that *"comprendre c'est pardonner."* We pardon because in understanding we have found another outlet for our thwarted will; the outlet of punishing is superfluous.

The scientist is not revengeful, nor, let us note incidentally, is he an ascetic—other forms of self-direction are more pleasing to him. He is not a social reformer. Social reform, however, is one of the great fields science is opening up to those whose energy is not diverted to scientific discovery or scientific order. As a region for applied science social reform is subject to the danger of scientific mistake. Perilous though this be to society, society runs a far greater risk through the popularisation of the idea that it may be scientifically developed. Once the applications of science get under way in society there is no telling the length

they might be put.   Modern mechanisms of war
might be but petty horrors compared to the under-
takings of social reformers, rampant in attempts
to control people "scientifically," to control birth
and death, to regulate mating, to control feeling
and thought and will, personality itself.   The
tyranny of traditional morality might be insignificant compared with that of the morality of
eugenics.   With the will to power of the social
reformer unrestrained, his zeal for scientific
management untempered, many of the subject
classes would be re-victimised—children, women,
the defectives and the criminal,[1] "backward"
peoples.   Once a progressive god is imagined, he
too will be enslaved to the determination to improve the race.   For such a progressive deity
theories of evolutionary culture have paved the
way.   Culture as a self-developing entity is an
embryonic god.[2]

[1] Consider the Pennsylvania law withholding a marriage license
from a man who has been within five years the inmate of a poor-
house unless he give proof of being able to support a family, or
the Nebraska law for the sterilisation of criminals "of confirmed
criminal tendencies." (*Social Hygiene*, April, 1916.)

[2] *See* Parsons, E. C., "A Progressive God," *The New Review*,
June, 1916.

With or without the aid of metaphysics, unless
our culture does develop along certain lines, prin-
cipally along the line of a greater tolerance for the
individual variation, a greater respect for personality, scientific applications to society may
indeed prove unimaginable tyranny.   Aside from
this possible turn of culture, however, there is
another social relief in sight.   Applied science
·will be concentrated more and more upon nature.
This diversion of energy from controlling the animate or the moral to controlling the inanimate or
the non-moral is in fact in process; it is already
one of the most characteristic features of modern
life.[1]   Thanks to the mechanical inventions it
resulted in, it has led to innumerable new fields
of work and play—for children, for women, and
for other subject classes.   It is transforming child-
bearing and the education of children.   It has

[1] It has been eloquently described by Walter Lippmann in
referring to the "practical" men who have come in contact with
the scientific method.   In them, he writes, "the instincts of
workmanship, of control over brute things, the desire for
order, the satisfaction of services rendered and uses created,
the civilising passions are given a chance to temper the primal
desire to have and to hold and to conquer."   (*Drift and Mastery*,
p. 49.)

meant public hygiene. Some day it may mean
social art. It has transformed belief in the
mystical efficacy of staying home into concern
over home conditions. It has meant improving
neighbourhoods (rather than regulating neighbours). It has directed attention from the ethics
of proprietorship to the ethics of use. It has
meant the preservation of natural resources, sub-
stituting here as elsewhere the idea of collective
ownership for the theory of natural rights and
private property. It has meant a world-wide
system of communication and transportation.
Some day it will mean industrial democracy.
Some day it will mean the disappearance of na-
tionalisation as it is now understood and the disappearance of national wars. Through lessening
interest not only in political boundaries but in all
social boundaries it will force a condition of
greater social tolerance in general, precluding the
individual from masking an attitude of arrogance
or tyranny under a social classification. In it,
in the concentration of our energy upon bettering
nature rather than upon bettering man, or, shall
we say, in bettering human beings through better-

ing the conditions they live under, in such outlets for effort and ambition I find the opportunity *par excellence* for a greater measure of social freedom.

# INDEX

Adoption, 21, 64 n. 1
Adultery, 40, 47, 48, 52, 63, 99, 168 n. 1
African peoples, 43 n. 2, 46, 58, 66 n. 2, 101 n. 1, 111, 112–13, 115–16, 117, 120, 127 n. 1, 128, 139, 155, 169. *See* Akikuyu, Wataveta
Age, 1, 6, 7, 37, 98 n. 1, 131, 152, 153
Age-classes, 2–3, 5, 7, 9, 27 ff., 60, 66 n. 1, 71 n. 2, 99, 101 n. 1, 108 n. 1, 115, 127 n. 1, 130 n. 1, 131, 139, 163, 166, 171, 172
Akikuyu, 13 n. 1, 118, 167
American colonies, 70 n. 1, 78, 95–6, 102
American Indians, 6, 7, 15, 25, 26, 30 n. 3, 41 n. 1, 42–3, 60, 64 n. 1, 69 n. 2, 95–6, 102, 116 n. 3, 128, 129, 132, 133 n. 1, 140, 157–8, 161–2, 163, 169. *See* Zuñi
Anglo-Saxons, 2 n. 3, 29 n. 1, 88 n. 1, 156, 157
Animals, 7, 9, 14, 15, 30 n. 3, 36, 62, 64, 69 n. 4, 102, 108 n. 1, 110 ff., 121, 127, 130 n.1, 135, 161, 162, 168, 171, 173 n. 2
Army, 5, 6, 19, 32, 72, n. 1, 124, 154 n. 1, 171, 172 n. 2
Art, 118 n. 1, 178
Asceticism, 145, 154, 156 ff., 169, 175

Backward peoples, 66 n. 1, 71 n. 2, 86 ff., 172, 176
Bahamas, 15, 120, 125
Barrenness, 12–14, 21, 36, 115, 168

Birth, 12, 17, 18–19, 22, 121, 176. *See* Pregnancy, Reproduction
Blackfellows, 13 n. 1, 26, 34, 37, 50, 69 n. 4, 111, 129 n. 1, 168 n. 1
Branding, 9, 25, 46, 100, 105 n. 1, 116
Breeding, 9, 10, 12–13, 36–7, 46, 60, 109, 116, 135, 168. *See* Impregnation
Buddhism, 93–4, 133–4

Caste, 1, 3, 6, 19, 69 n. 2, 76–9, 83 n. 1, 88 n. 1, 108 n. 1, 132 n. 2, 163, 166, 170, 172. *See* Chiefs, Servants, Slaves
Celibacy, 9 n. 1, 36, 115, 127, 137
Ceremonialism, 5–6, 13, 16–17, 24, 25, 32, 36 n. 1, 37 n. 1, 50, 58, 69 n. 1, 91, 94, 107, 112–13, 124 ff.
Chiefs, 3 n. 1, 9 n. 1, 13 n. 1, 19, 24, 32, 36, 37, 64 n. 1, 69 n. 1, n. 4, 80 n. 2, 108, 109, 113 n. 2, 119, 124, 127 n. 1, 135–9, 152 n. 1, 158, 160–1, 165, 167, 170 n. 2
Children, 10, 20, 34, 35, 47, 62, 114–15, 118 n. 1, 134, 167, 176, 177. *See* Parents
Chinese, 46 n. 2, 50, 63 n. 3, 91–2, 93, 107, 111, 128, 131 n. 1, 132 n. 1, 140–1, 155, 159–60, 162, 169
Chivalry, 51, 172
Christianity, 5, 36, 93–4, 104 n. 1, 107, 112 n. 1, 128, 132, 133–4, 142–3, 144, 147, 154 n. 1, 156, 160, 161 n. 1, 163, 173 n. 2

# Index